ONTARIO
POLICE REVIEW

Complete Ontario Police Constable Study Guide and Practice Test Questions

COMPLETE
TEST PREPARATION INC.
WWW.TEST-PREPARATION.CA

Pass the Ontario Police!

Copyright © 2018 Complete Test Preparation Inc. ALL RIGHTS RESERVED.

No part of this book may be reproduced or transferred in any form or by any means, graphic, electronic, or mechanical, including photocopying, recording, web distribution, taping, or by any information storage retrieval system, without the written permission of the author.

Notice: Complete Test Preparation Inc. makes every reasonable effort to obtain from reliable sources accurate, complete, and timely information about the tests covered in this book. Nevertheless, changes can be made in the tests or the administration of the tests at any time and Complete Test Preparation Inc. makes no representation or warranty, either expressed or implied as to the accuracy, timeliness, or completeness of the information contained in this book. Complete Test Preparation Inc. make no representations or warranties of any kind, express or implied, about the completeness, accuracy, reliability, suitability or availability with respect to the information contained in this document for any purpose. Any reliance you place on such information is therefore strictly at your own risk.

The author(s) shall not be liable for any loss incurred as a consequence of the use and application, directly or indirectly, of any information presented in this work. Sold with the understanding, the author is not engaged in rendering professional services or advice. If advice or expert assistance is required, the services of a competent professional should be sought.

The company, product and service names used in this publication are for identification purposes only. All trademarks and registered trademarks are the property of their respective owners. Complete Test Preparation Inc. is not affiliated with any educational institution.

Complete Test Preparation Inc. is not affiliated with the Ontario Ministry of Correctional Services, who were not involved in the production of, and does not endorse, this product.

We strongly recommend that students check with exam providers for up-to-date information regarding test content.

ISBN-13: 9781772450774

Version 7.8 November 2020

Published by
Complete Test Preparation Inc.
Victoria BC Canada
Visit us on the web at https://www.test-preparation.ca
Printed in the USA

About Complete Test Preparation Inc.

The Complete Test Preparation Team has been publishing high quality study materials since 2005. Over one million students from all over the world visit our websites every year, and thousands of students, teachers and parents all over the world (over 100 countries) have purchased our teaching materials, curriculum, study guides and practice tests.

Complete Test Preparation is committed to providing students with the best study materials and practice tests available on the market. Members of our team combine years of teaching experience, with experienced writers and editors, all with advanced degrees.

Feedback

We welcome your feedback. Email us at feedback@test-preparation.ca with your comments and suggestions. We carefully review all suggestions and often incorporate reader suggestions into upcoming versions. As a Print on Demand Publisher, we update our products frequently.

CONTENTS

6   **Getting Started**
- How this study guide is organized   7
- The Police Constable Study Plan   8
- Making a Study Schedule   10

15   **Police Analytical Thinking Inventory (PATI)**
- PATI Self-Assessment   16
- **Section I - Logic**   19
- Syllogism Self Assessment   19
- Answer Key   21
- Logic – A Quick Tutorial   21
- **Section II - Mapping**   29
- Mapping Self-Assessment   29
- Answer Key   33

34   **Part II - Inductive Reasoning**
- **Section I - Matching**   34
- Matching Self-Assessment   35
- Answer Key   38
- How to Answer Matching Questions   39
- **Section II - Sequences**   41
- Sequences Self-Assessment   42
- Answer Key   45

46   **Part III - Quantitative Reasoning**
- **Section I - Basic Math**   46
- Basic Math Self-Assessment   47
- Answer Key   52
- Fraction Tips, Tricks and Shortcuts   54
- Decimals Tips, Tricks and Shortcuts   55
- Converting Decimals to Fractions   59
- Percent Tips, Tricks and Shortcuts   60
- How to Answer Basic Math Multiple Choice   62
- Basic Math Multiple Choice Strategy   63

67 **Section II - Problem Solving**
        Self-Assessment   68
        Answer Key   72
        How to Solve Word Problems   73
        Types of Word Problems   76

85 **Written Communication Summary (WCT)**
        WCT Self-Assessment   86
        Main Idea and Supporting Details   91

94 **Practice Test Questions Set 1**
        Answer Key   129

142 **Practice Test Questions Set 2**
        Answer Key   178

190 **Conclusion**

Getting Started

CONGRATULATIONS! By deciding to take the Ontario Police Constable, you have taken the first step toward a great future! Of course, there is no point in taking this important examination unless you intend to do your best to earn the highest grade you possibly can. That means getting yourself organized and discovering the best approaches, methods and strategies to master the material. Yes, that will require real effort and dedication, but if you are willing to focus your energy and devote the study time necessary, before you know it you will be on you way to a brighter future!

We know that taking on a new endeavour can be scary, and it is easy to feel unsure of where to begin. That's where we come in. This study guide is designed to help you improve your test-taking skills, show you a few tricks of the trade and increase both your competency and confidence.

The Ontario Police Constable Test

The Ontario Police Constable test is composed of three sections as follows:

Part 1 - Police Analytical Thinking Inventory (PATI)

This section includes three areas:

- **Deductive Reasoning** - Logic Questions (syllogisms) map reading questions.

- **Inductive Reasoning** - Classification and Picture Series questions

- **Quantitative Reasoning** - Basic math and math problem solving (Word Problems) questions.

Part II - Written Communication Test (WCT)

This section tests your ability to order and present information in a logical fashion. Students are typically given a short passage where the information may be scrambled chronologically and are asked to summarize.

While we seek to make our guide as comprehensive as possible, note that like all exams, the Ontario Police Constable test might be adjusted at some future point. New material might be added, or content that is no longer relevant or applicable might be removed. It is always a good idea to give the materials you receive when you register to take the Ontario Police Constable test a careful review.

How This Study Guide Is Organized

This study guide is divided into three sections. The first section, Self-Assessments, which will help you recognize your areas of strength and weaknesses. This will be a boon when it comes to managing your study time the most efficiently; there is not much point of focusing on material you have already got firmly under control. Instead, taking the self-assessments will show you where that time could be much better spent. In this area you will begin with a few questions to evaluate quickly your understanding of material that is likely to appear on the test. If you do poorly in certain areas, simply work carefully through those sections in the tutorials and then try the self-assessment again.

The second section, Tutorials, offers information in each of the content areas, as well as strategies to help you master that material. The tutorials are not intended to be a complete course, but cover general principles. If you find that you do not understand the tutorials, it is recommended that you seek out additional instruction.

Third, we offer two sets of practice test questions, similar to those on the exam.

The Police Constable Study Plan

Now that you have made the decision to take the Police Constable test, it is time to get started. Before you do another thing, you will need to figure out a plan of attack. The best study tip is to start early! The longer the time period you devote to regular study practice, the likelier you will be to retain the material and be able to access it quickly. If you thought that 1x20 is the same as 2x10, guess what? It really is not, when it comes to study time. Reviewing material for just an hour per day over the course of 20 days is far better than studying for two hours a day for only 10 days. The more often you revisit a particular piece of information, the better you will know it. Not only will your grasp and understanding be better, but your ability to reach into your brain and quickly and efficiently pull out the tidbit you need, will be greatly enhanced as well.

The great Chinese scholar and philosopher Confucius believed that true knowledge could be defined as knowing what you know and what you do not know. The first step in preparing for the Police Constable test is to assess your strengths and weaknesses. You may already have an idea of what you know and what you do not know, but evaluating yourself using our Self- Assessment modules for each of the test content areas.

Making a Study Schedule

To make your study time the most productive you will need to develop a study plan. The purpose of the plan is to organize all the bits of pieces of information in such a way that you will not feel overwhelmed. Rome was not built in a day, and learning everything you will need to know to pass the Police Constable is going to take time, too. Arranging the material you need to learn into manageable chunks is the best way to go. Each study session should make you feel as though you have accomplished your goal, or at least are closer, and your goal is simply to learn what you planned to learn during that particular session. Try to organize the content in such a way that each study session builds on previous ones. That way, you will retain the information, be better able to access it, and review the previous bits and pieces at the same time.

Self-assessment

The Best Study Tip! The best study tip is to start early! The longer you study regularly, the more you will retain and 'learn' the material. Studying for 1 hour per day for 20 days is far better than studying for 2 hours for 10 days.

What don't you know?

The first step is to assess your strengths and weaknesses. You may already have an idea of where your weaknesses are, or you can take our Self-assessment modules for each of the content areas.

Exam Component	Rate 1 to 5
Inductive Reasoning	
Classification	
Picture Series	
Deductive Reasoning	
Logic	
Map Reading	
Quantitative Reasoning	
Basic Math	
Percent	
Decimals	
Word Problems	

Making a Study Schedule

The key to making a study plan is to divide the material you need to learn into manageable sized pieces and learn it, while at the same time reviewing the material that you already know.

Using the table above, any scores of 3 or below, you need to spend time learning, reviewing and practicing this subject area. A score of 4 means you need to review the material, but you don't have to spend time re-learning. A score of 5 and you are OK with just an occasional review before the exam.

A score of 0 or 1 means you really need to work on this should allocate the most time and the highest priority.

Some students prefer a 5-day plan and others a 10-day plan. It also depends on how much time until the exam.

Here is an example of a 5-day plan based on an example from the table above:

Picture Series: 1- Study 1 hour everyday – review on last day
Map Reading: 3 - Study 1 hour for 3 days then ½ hour a day, then review
Word Problems: 4 - Review every second day
Classification: 5 - Review for ½ hour every other day
Logic: 5 - Review for ½ hour every other day

Using this example, Logic and Classification are good, and only need occasional review. Map Reading is good and needs 'some' review. Picture Series is very weak and need most of your time. Based on this, here is a sample study plan:

Day	Subject	Time
Monday		
Study	Picture Series	1 hour
Study	Word Problems	1 hour
½ hour break		
Study	Map Reading	1 hour
Review	Reading Comp.	½ hour
Tuesday		
Study	Picture Series	1 hour
Study	Word Problems	½ hour
½ hour break		
Study	Map Reading	½ hour
Review	Classification	½ hour
Review	Logic	½ hour
Wednesday		
Study	Picture Series	1 hour
Study	Word Problems	½ hour
½ hour break		
Study	Map Reading	½ hour
Review	Picture Series	½ hour
Thursday		
Study	Picture Series	½ hour
Study	Word Problems	½ hour
Review	Map Reading	½ hour
½ hour break		
Review	Logic	½ hour
Review	Classification	½ hour
Friday		
Review	Picture Series	½ hour
Review	Word Problems	½ hour
Review	Map Reading	½ hour
½ hour break		
Review	Classification	½ hour
Review	Logic	½ hour

Using this example, adapt the study plan to your own schedule. This schedule assumes 2 ½ - 3 hours available to study everyday for a 5 day period.

First, write out what you need to study and how much. Next figure out how many days before the test. Note, do NOT study on the last day before the test. On the last day before the test, you won't learn anything and will probably only confuse yourself.

Make a table with the days before the test and the number of hours you have available to study each day. We suggest working with 1 hour and ½ hour time slots.

Start filling in the blanks, with the subjects you need to study the most, getting the most time, and the most regular time slots (i.e. everyday) and the subjects that you know getting the least time (e.g. ½ hour every other day, or every 3rd day).

Tips for making a schedule

Once you make a schedule, stick with it! Make your study sessions reasonable. If you make a study schedule and don't stick with it, you set yourself up for failure. Instead, schedule study sessions that are a bit shorter and set yourself up for success! Make sure your study sessions are do-able. Studying is hard work, but after you pass, you can party and take a break!

Schedule breaks. Breaks are just as important as study time. Work out a rotation of studying and breaks that works for you.

Build up study time. If you find it hard to sit still and study for 1 hour straight through, build up to it. Start with 20 minutes, and then take a break. Once you get used to 20-minute study sessions, increase the time to 30 minutes. Gradually work you way up to 1 hour.

How to Make a Study Plan and Schedule
https://www.test-preparation.ca/make-study-plan/

40 minutes to 1 hour is optimal. Studying for longer than this is tiring and not productive. Studying for shorter isn't long enough to be productive.

Studying Math. Studying Math is different from studying other subjects because you use a different part of your brain. The best way to study math is to practice everyday. This will train your mind to think in a mathematical way. If you miss a day or days, the mathematical mind-set is gone, and you have to start all over again to build it up.

More on how to study math
https://www.test-preparation.ca/how-to-study-for-a-math-test-the-complete-guide/

How to Study
For more information, see our How to Study Guide at
https://www.test-preparation.ca/learning-study/
For additional information on getting organized to study, see our How to Study book at www.study-skills.ca.

Analytical Thinking Inventory PATI

THIS SECTION CONTAINS A SELF-ASSESSMENT AND TUTORIAL. The tutorials are designed to familiarize general principles and the self-assessment contains general questions similar to the PATI questions likely to be on the Police Constable exam, but are not intended to be identical. The tutorials are not designed to be a complete course, and it is assumed that students have some familiarity with this type of material. If you do not understand parts of the tutorials, or find the tutorials difficult, it is recommended that you seek out additional instruction.

Tour of the PATI Content

Below is a detailed list of the types of reading questions that generally appear on your exam.

- Drawing logical conclusions (Syllogisms)
- Reading simple maps and making calculations
- Basic Math including fractions, decimals, percent, simple equations and arithmetic
- Word problems
- Classify similar objects
- Recognize series and common features

The questions below are not the same as you will find on the exam - that would be too easy! And nobody knows what the questions will be and they change all the time. Mostly the changes consist of substituting new questions for old, but the changes can be new question formats or styles, changes to the number of questions in each section, changes to the time limits for each section and combining sections. Below are general reading and vocabulary questions that cover the same areas as the exam. So the format and exact wording of the questions may differ slightly, and change from year to year, if you can answer the questions below, you will have no problem with the PATI section of the test.

PATI Self-Assessment

The purpose of the self-assessment is:

- Identify your strengths and weaknesses.
- Develop your personalized study plan (above)
- Get accustomed to the Police Constable test format
- Extra practice – the self-assessments are almost a full 3rd practice test!
- Provide a baseline score for preparing your study schedule.

Once complete, use the table below to assess your understanding of the content, and prepare your study schedule described in chapter 1.

80% - 100%	Excellent – you have mastered the content
60 – 79%	Good. You have a working knowledge. Even though you can just pass this section, you may want to review the tutorials and do some extra practice to see if you can improve your mark.
40% - 59%	Below Average. You do not understand reading comprehension problems. Review the tutorials , and retake this quiz again in a few days, before proceeding to the Practice Test Questions.
Less than 40%	Poor. You have a very limited understanding of reading comprehension problems. Please review the tutorials , and retake this quiz again in a few days, before proceeding to the Practice Test Questions.

PART I - DEDUCTIVE REASONING SYLLOGISMS AND MAPPING

	A	B	C	D
1	○	○	○	○
2	○	○	○	○
3	○	○	○	○
4	○	○	○	○
5	○	○	○	○
6	○	○	○	○
7	○	○	○	○
8	○	○	○	○
9	○	○	○	○
10	○	○	○	○

Section I - Logic

Syllogism Self Assessment

1. The Silver fish can swim faster than the black fish. The gold fish can swim faster than the black fish. The gold fish can swim faster than the silver fish.

If the first 2 statements are true, then the third statement is:

   a. True
   b. False
   c. Uncertain

2. All rabbits have fur. Some rabbits are pets. Some pets have fur. If the first 2 statements are true, then the third statement is:

   a. True
   b. False
   c. Uncertain

3. Deciduous trees drop their leaves in the fall. Conifers keep their leaves all year round. Conifers are deciduous. If the first 2 statements are true, then the third statement is:

   a. True
   b. False
   c. Uncertain

4. No homework is fun. Reading is homework. Reading is not fun. If the first 2 statements are true, then the third statement is:

    a. True
    b. False
    c. Uncertain

5. All informative things are useful things. Some websites are not useful things. Some websites are not informative. If the first 2 statements are true, then the third statement is:

    a. True
    b. False
    c. Uncertain

Answer Key

1. Uncertain
We don't have enough information here to make a decision. Perhaps the gold fish can swim faster than the black fish AND the silver fish – we don't know.

2. True
This argument is a little sloppy, because the 2nd statement and the conclusion both use 'some.' However, it is a valid argument.

3. False
This is a clearly false argument.

4. True
This is a very strong argument. If the first two statement are true, then the third statement or conclusion must be true.

5. True
This is a strong argument since the first statement uses 'all,' and the second statement uses 'some.' And the conclusion uses 'some.'

Logic - A Quick Tutorial

Understanding syllogism can be tricky which is why it's important to understand the strategies involved in solving the problems. Here are some tips to guide you when reviewing for syllogism exam questions:

Logical syllogisms have three key components: the major premise, minor premise, and the conclusion. Practicing logic questions helps you identify these quickly and easily.

There are two terms used in each part, which can be understood through the form "'Some/all A is/are [not] B." Each premise has a common term with the conclusion as seen in the example below:

Premise: All birds are animals
Premise: All parrots are birds
Conclusion: All parrots are animals

In this example, "animal" is the major term and predicate of the conclusion, "parrot" is the minor term and subject of the conclusion, and "bird" is the middle term.

Clearly, this argument is rock-solid. If ALL birds are animals, AND all parrots are birds, then the conclusion must be true – All parrots must be animals.

To check on this, let's try a variation:

Some birds are animals.
All parrots are birds
All parrots are animals.

Clearly, this is not true. If only 'some' birds are animals, then there are some birds which are NOT animals, and we don't have any information about if the 'some' birds which are not animals. Perhaps the 'some birds that are not animals' are parrots, and perhaps not.

Here is another example:

This store only sells used textbooks.
My textbook is used.
My textbook came from that store.

This is clearly a not true. We do not know if the store is the only store in the world that sells textbooks, so clearly the textbook in question could have come from that store or any other store.

STRUCTURE

There are four possible variations to each "Some/all/no A is/are [not] B," structure.

All birds are animals.
All parrots are birds.
All parrots are animals.

Clearly a very solid argument – IF all birds are animals AND all parrots are birds, then the conclusion, all parrots are animals MUST be true.

Here is a variation that is NOT true:

Some birds are animals.
All parrots are birds.
All parrots are animals.

Here we don't know if the 'some' birds that are NOT animals includes parrots or not. They may be but we don't know.

Here is the negative example:

No birds are foxes.
All parrots are birds.
No parrots are foxes.

A very good argument where the conclusion, No parrots are foxes MUST be true if the premises are true.

Notice what happens if we substitute 'some' into the argument.

Some birds are foxes.
All parrots are birds.
No parrots are foxes.

No birds are foxes.
Some parrots are birds.
No parrots are foxes.

Both of these are clearly false. The argument relies on the fact the absolute statements ALL and NONE.

Using some can give a very solid argument though.
Consider these:
All dogs are animals.

Some mammals are dogs.
Some mammals are animals.

No dogs are birds.
Some mammals are dogs.
Some mammals are not birds.

No restaurant food is healthy.
Some recipes are healthy.
Some recipes are not restaurant foods.

All liars are evildoers.
Some doctors are not evildoers.
Some doctors are not liars.

All these are very good arguments where the conclusion MUST be true if the premises are true.

Below is a comprehensive list of all valid logic argument forms. Study these forms and make sure that you are familiar with them and understand why the conclusion must be true.

The Real World

Generally, exam questions are not exactly like the forms we have been discussing so far, but are similar. Understanding the correct forms is still very important and necessary to understanding the underlying structure.
Here are some example logic questions:

1.
Practice makes perfect.
I am perfect.
I practiced a lot.

If the first 2 statements are true, then the third statement is:

True   False   Uncertain
The correct answer is - Uncertain. There are all sorts of

reasons you could be perfect without practicing. For example, you could be perfect looking, or your hair could be perfect, or you could be perfect by a coincidence.

2.
People who smoke cigarettes have a 75% chance of getting cancer.

I have cancer.
I smoked a lot.

If the first 2 statements are true, then the third statement is:

True   False   Uncertain

The correct answer is - Uncertain. There are many reasons you could have cancer. In addition, you may be among the 25% of people who smoke and do NOT get cancer.

3.
Most car accidents happen in the morning.
I don't drive in the morning.
I am unlikely to have an accident.
If the first 2 statements are true, then the third statement is:

True   False   Uncertain
The correct answer is - Uncertain.

4.
Halibut are a large fish.
I caught a small fish.
I did not catch a halibut.
If the first 2 statements are true, then the third statement is:

True   False   Uncertain

The correct answer is – False. You could have caught a baby halibut. In order for this to be true, you would have to say,

All halibut are large fish.
I caught a small fish.
I did not catch a halibut.
Here, the first premise is ALL halibut are large, which would

include baby halibut, so if the first two premises are true, the third statement MUST be true also.

A Different Style

Here is a different style of question.

1.
Angel gets the highest grades in all the subjects in school. She is also the president of the Student Council. Every year she gets the highest award given by the school.

    a. Angel is a slow learner.

    b. Everybody admires Angel.

    c. Other children are envious of Angel.

    d. Angel is at the top of her class.

Let's look at the choices. Choice A is clearly false. Choice B, may be true but it also may not be true – no information is given. It is likely that everyone admires her, but we don't know that for sure. The same with choice C. Probably other students are envious of her, but we don't know that for sure and no information is given. She could, for example, have rigged the election for Student Council and cheated on all her exams and everyone hates her!
Choice D is correct – This we do now for sure.

2.
Students enjoy playing football after school. Sometimes, they play basketball with other kids. On weekends, they play baseball, badminton, or tennis.

    a. Students prefer playing indoors.

    b. Students enjoy different kinds of sports.

    c. Students hate playing.

    d. Playing is a form of exercise.

The correct answer is B. The only certain thing is children enjoy different kinds of sports. For choice A, no information is given if they are playing indoors or outdoors. Choice C is probably false, but we don't know. Choice D is true, but not related to the information given. Choice D is designed to confuse.

List of all Valid Logic Argument forms

All men are fallible.
All men are animals.
Some animals are fallible.

Some books are precious.
All books are perishable.
Some perishable things are precious.

All books are imperfect.
Some books are informative.
Some informative things are imperfect.

No snakes are good to eat.
All snakes are animals.
Some animals are not good to eat.

Some websites are not helpful.
All websites are internet resources.
Some internet resources are not helpful.

No lepers are allowed to enter the church.
All lepers are human.
Some humans are not allowed to enter the church.

All pigs are unclean.
All unclean things are best avoided.
Some things that are best avoided are pigs.

All trees are plants.
No plants are birds.
No birds are trees.

Some evil doers are lawyers.
All lawyers are human.
Some humans are evil doers.

No meals are free.
All free things are desirable.
Some desirable things are not meals.

No dogs are birds.
Some birds are pets.
Some pets are not dogs.

Section II - Mapping

Mapping Self-Assessment

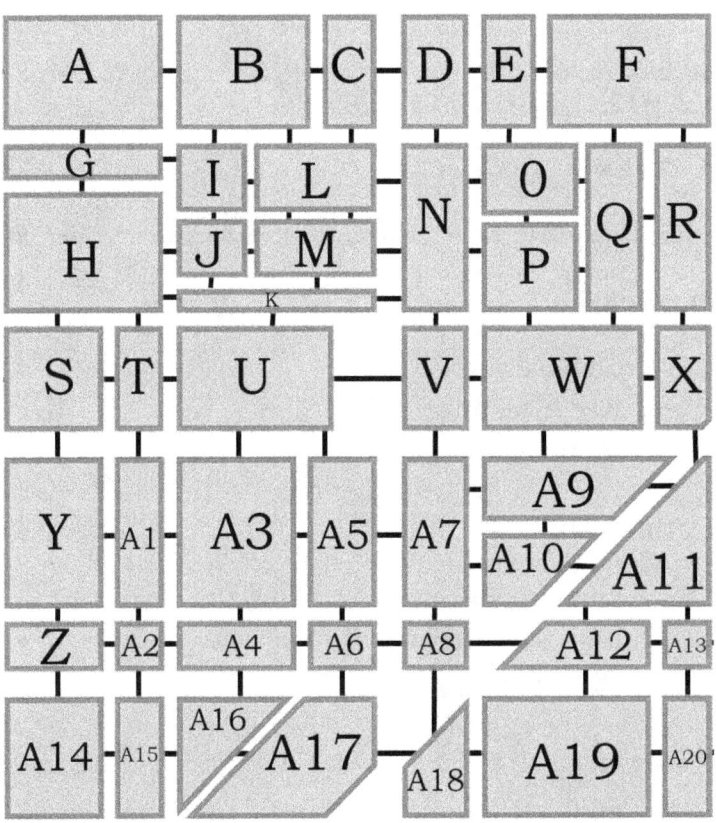

MAP KEY

Each square labeled A to Z and A1 to A20, represent the corner of an intersection. The lines between the squares represent a city block. The intersections and city blocks fall under 3 categories.

Large blocks: A, B,F, H, N, Q, R, U, W, Y, A3, A5, A7, A9, A11, A14, A17, A19

Small blocks: C, D, E, I. J, L,M, O, P, S, T, V, X, A1, A4, A10, Z, A12, A15, A16, A18, A20

Mini blocks: G, K, A2, A6, A8, A13

The time it takes to travel from one city block to another is:

Large blocks

    In a car: 4 minutes
    On a bike: 6 minutes
    On foot: 10 minutes

Small Blocks

    In a car: 3 minutes
    On a bike: 5 minutes
    On foot: 8 minutes

Mini Blocks

    In a car: 2 minutes
    On a bike: 4 minutes
    On foot: 6 minutes

6. What is the shortest time it would take a woman to go from block A to S driving a car?

   a. 11 minutes
   b. 7 and half minutes
   c. 8 minutes
   d. 10 minutes

7. What is the shortest time it would take a man to go from A to S if he drove the first two blocks, then rode a bike the rest of the way?

   a. 18 minutes
   b. 16 minutes
   c. 17 minutes
   d. 15 minutes

8. A student has to walk home from block U to R. What is the shortest time it would take him if he had to go through block Q?

   a. 38 minutes
   b. 32 minutes
   c. 37 minutes
   d. 29 minutes

9. A police patrol car in block Y has to respond to a call in Block G. How fast can they get there if they are forced by traffic to avoid Block S?

   a. 20 minutes
   b. 19 minutes
   c. 14 minutes
   d. 17 minutes

10. How fast would it take a man on bike to ride from block Z to block A7 if he had to spend two minutes and half along the way fixing his bike?

  a. 22. 5 minutes
  b. 22 minutes
  c. 24.5 minutes
  d. 24 minutes

Answer Key

6. D
The shortest route would take a car through A – G – H - S, covering two large blocks and one mini block. This would take 10 minutes by car.

7. B
The shortest route from A to S is A – G – H – S, taking 6 minutes by car for the first 2 blocks and 10 minutes on a bike for the last large block. Total time is 16 minutes.

8. A
The shortest route from U to R passing through Q is U – V – W – Q – R. Time to walk these blocks is 38 minutes. (A)

9. C
The shortest route from block Y to G, avoiding S, is Y – A1 – T – H – G. Time by car is 14 minutes.

10. C
The fastest route is Z – A2 – A4 – A6 – A8 – A7. Time by bike is 22 minutes, plus 2.5 minutes to fix the bike, for a total of 24.5 minutes.

Part II - Inductive Reasoning
Section I - Matching

	A	B	C	D
1	○	○	○	○
2	○	○	○	○
3	○	○	○	○
4	○	○	○	○
5	○	○	○	○
6	○	○	○	○
7	○	○	○	○
8	○	○	○	○
9	○	○	○	○
10	○	○	○	○

Directions: In each of the following questions, select the choice that does not belong with the other three.

1.

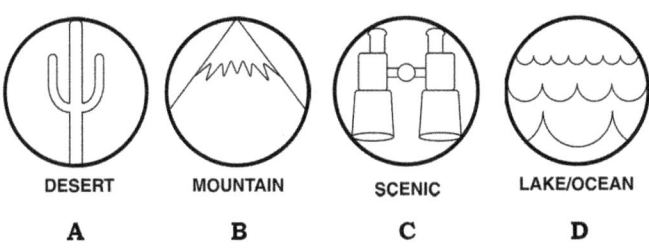

2.

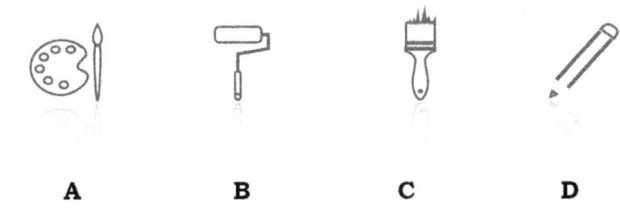

3.

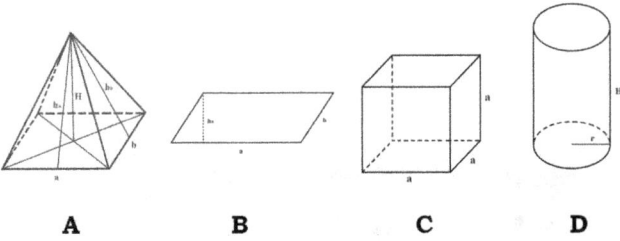

4.

AB MN PR XY
   A   B   C   D

5.

   A   B   C   D

6.

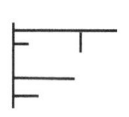 

   A   B   C   D

7.

7   13   17   14
   A   B   C   D

8.

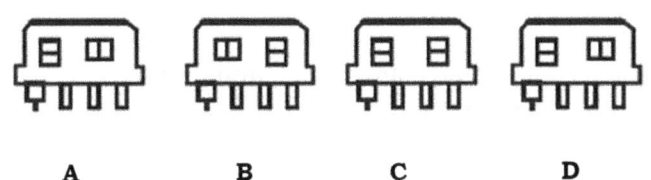

A B C D

9.

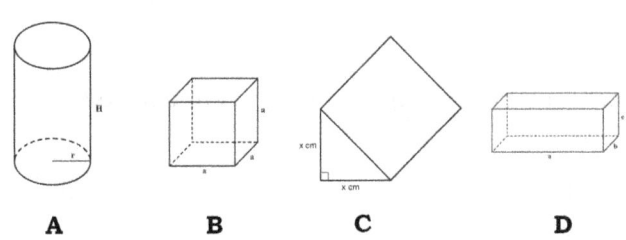

A B C D

10.

O I T X

A B C D

Answer Key

1. C
All the choices describe a geographical landform except Choice C which describes a 'scenic' place.

2. D
All the choices are connected with paint, except choice D.

3. B
All the choices are 3-dimensional figures except choice B.

4. C
All the choices are consecutive letters except choice C.

5. B
All the choice have an even number of sides except choice B.

6. C
All the choice have a vertical line as the longest except C.

7. D
All the choice are prime numbers except choice D.

8. C
All the choices have a rotated rectangle except choice C.

9. A
All the choices have straight edges on all sides except choice A.

10. A
All the choice are composed of straight lines except choice A.

How to Answer Matching Questions

Answering this type of question is a skill that can be learned mainly through practice, and familiarizing yourself with the different types of relationships you will likely find.

Here is a list of relationships you are likely to find:

Numbers: Look for the following:

- Prime numbers
- Consecutive numbers
- Simple addition, subtraction, multiplication or division (e.g. 10, 20, 30, or e.g. 27, 9, 81 are all divisible by 3)
- Fractions - Lowest common form, reciprocals

Letters: Look for the following:

- Consecutive letters
- Shape of letters
- Sound of letters

Purpose: This means that 'A' is used for 'B' and 'C' but not for 'D."

Cause and Effect: This means that 'A' has an effect on 'B' and 'C' but not for 'D.'

Part to Whole (individual to group): This means that 'A' is a part of 'B' and 'C' but not for 'D.'

Part to part: 'A,' 'B' and 'C' are parts of something which 'D' is not.

Action to object: 'A' is done to 'B' and 'C' but not to 'D.'

Types - look for types of transport, sports, animals

- **Dots and Shading:** Any dots or shadings that look even

slightly different will almost certainly be part of the answer.

• **Geometric figures:** Look for the number sides, shading, borders, relation between the inside and border etc.

• **Place:** 'A,' 'B' and 'C' are related places and choice 'D' is not.

Inductive Reasoning Section II - Sequences

	A	B	C	D
1	○	○	○	○
2	○	○	○	○
3	○	○	○	○
4	○	○	○	○
5	○	○	○	○
6	○	○	○	○
7	○	○	○	○
8	○	○	○	○
9	○	○	○	○
10	○	○	○	○

Directions: Choose the figure that completes the sequence.

1.

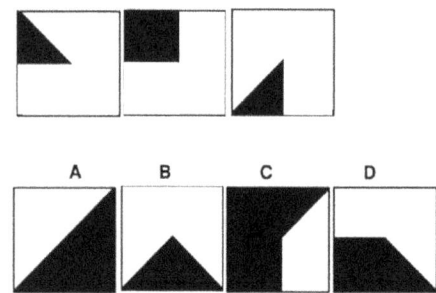

2.

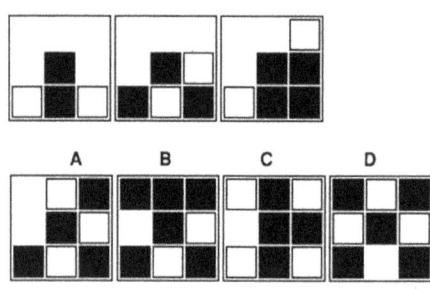

3.

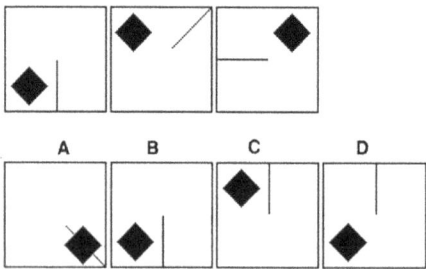

4.

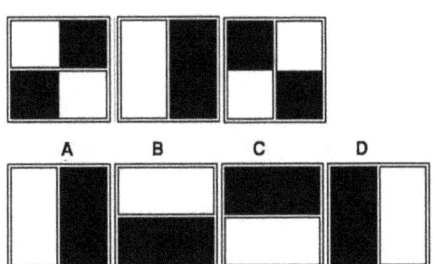

5.

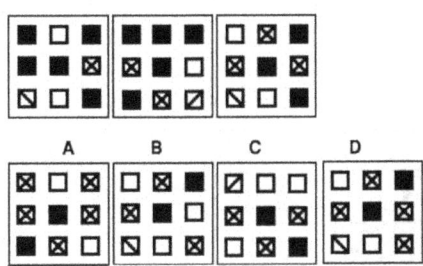

6.

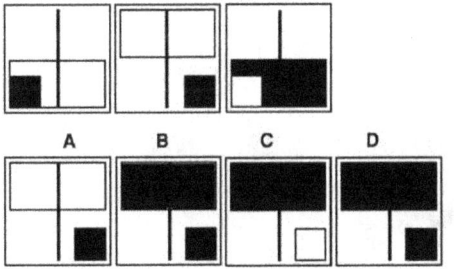

7.

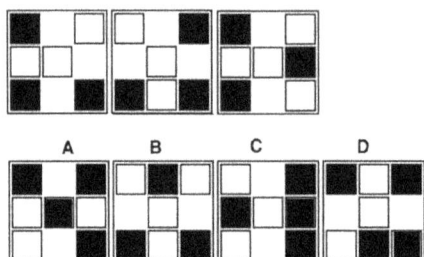

8.

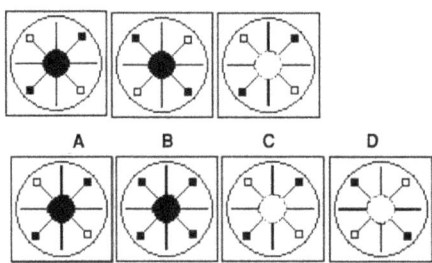

9.

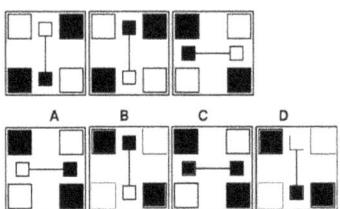

10.

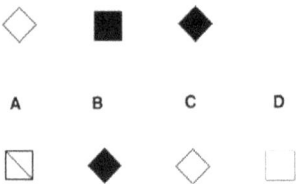

Answer Key

1. B
Each figure is created by adding the mirror image of the previous figure.

2. B
Each square has 2 blank squares.

3. A
The inner square is rotated clockwise on the corner of the outside square.

4. C
The bottom box is rotated counter-clockwise.

5. A
The colors of the two square boxes are reversed.

6. B
The sum of inside dots decreases by one.

7. D
The box is rotated and the shading reversed.

8. B
The number of sides increases by one.

9. B
The shape rotates clockwise.

10. D
The box is rotated and the shading reversed.

Part III - Quantitative Reasoning
Section I - Basic Math

	A	B	C	D
1	○	○	○	○
2	○	○	○	○
3	○	○	○	○
4	○	○	○	○
5	○	○	○	○
6	○	○	○	○
7	○	○	○	○
8	○	○	○	○
9	○	○	○	○
10	○	○	○	○
11	○	○	○	○
12	○	○	○	○
13	○	○	○	○
14	○	○	○	○
15	○	○	○	○
16	○	○	○	○
17	○	○	○	○
18	○	○	○	○
19	○	○	○	○
20	○	○	○	○

ANALYTICAL THINKING INVENTORY

1. 389 + 454 =

    a. 853
    b. 833
    c. 843
    d. 863

2. 9,177 + 7,204 =

    a. 16,4712
    b. 16,371
    c. 16,381
    d. 15,412

3. 2,199 + 5,832 =

    a. 8,331
    b. 8,041
    c. 8,141
    d. 8,031

4. 8,390 - 5,239 =

    a. 3,261
    b. 3,151
    c. 3,161
    d. 3,101

5. 643 - 587 =

    a. 56
    b. 66
    c. 46
    d. 55

6. 3,406 - 2,767 =

   a. 629
   b. 720
   c. 639
   d. 649

7. 149 × 7 =

   a. 1032
   b. 1043
   c. 1059
   d. 1063

8. 467 × 41 =

   a. 19,147
   b. 21,227
   c. 23,107
   d. 18,177

9. 309 × 17 =

   a. 5,303
   b. 4,913
   c. 4,773
   d. 5,253

10. 491 ÷ 9 =

    a. 54 r5
    b. 56 r6
    c. 57 r5
    d. 51 r

DECIMALS, FRACTIONS AND PERCENT

11. 15 is what percent of 200?

    a. 7.5%
    b. 15%
    c. 20%
    d. 17.50%

12. Add 10% of 300 to 50% of 20

    a. 50%
    b. 40%
    c. 60%
    d. 45%

13. Convert 90% to a fraction

    a. 1/10
    b. 9/9
    c. 10/100
    d. 9/10

14. Multiply 3 by 25% of 40

    a. 75
    b. 30
    c. 68
    d. 35

15. Convert 0.45 to a fraction

   a. 7/20
   b. 7/45
   c. 9/20
   d. 3/20

16. Convert 1/5 to percent.

   a. 10%
   b. 5%
   c. 20%
   d. 25%

17. Convert 4/20 to percent

   a. 25%
   b. 20%
   c. 40%
   d. 30%

18. Convert 0.55 to percent

   a. 45%
   b. 15%
   c. 75%
   d. 55%

19. Convert 0.33 to percent

   a. 77%
   b. 67%
   c. 33%
   d. 57%

20. A man buys an item for $420 and has a balance of $3000.00. How much did he have before?

    a. $2,580
    b. $3,420
    c. $2,420
    d. $342

Answer Key

Basic Math

1. C
389 + 454 = 843

2. C
9,177 + 7,204 = 16,381

3. D
2,199 + 5,832 = 8,031

4. B
8,390 - 5,239 = 3,151

5. A
643 - 587 = 56

6. C
3,406 - 2,767 = 639

7. B
149 × 7 = 1043

8. A
467 × 41 = 19,147

9. D
309 × 17 = 52,53

10. A
491 ÷ 9 = 54 r5

Decimals, Percent and Fractions

11. A
15% = 15/100 X 200 = 7.5%

12. B
10% of 300 = 30 and 50% of 20 = 10 so 30 + 1- = 40.

13. D
90% = 90/100 = 9/10

14. B
25% of 40 = 10 and 10 x 3 = 30

15. C
0.45 = 45/100 = 9/20

16. C
1/5 X 100 = 20%

17. B
4/20 X 100 = 1/5 X 100 = 20%

18. D
0.55 X 100 = 55%

19. C
0.33 X 100 = 33%

20. B
(Amount Spent) $420 + $3000 (Balance) = $3420

Basic Math Video Tutorials

Visit us online for the video version of these tutorials

https://www.test-preparation.ca/basic-math-video-tutorials/

Fraction Tips, Tricks and Shortcuts

When you are writing an exam, time is precious, so anything you can do to answer questions faster is a real advantage.

Here are some ideas, shortcuts, tips and tricks that can speed up answering fraction problems.

Remember that a fraction is just a number which names a portion of something. For instance, instead of having a whole pie, a fraction says you have a part of a pie--such as a half of one or a fourth of one.

Two numbers make up a fraction. The number on top is the numerator. The number on the bottom is the denominator.

To remember which is which, just remember that "denominator" and "down" both start with a "d." And the "downstairs" number is the denominator. So for instance, in ½, the numerator is 1, and the denominator (or "downstairs") number is 2.

Adding Fractions

It's easy to add two fractions if they have the same denominator. Just add the digits on top and leave the bottom one the same: 1/10 + 6/10 = 7/10.

It's the same with subtracting fractions with the same denominator: 7/10 - 6/10 = 1/10.

Adding and subtracting fractions with different denominators is a little more complicated.

First, you have to arrange the fractions so they have the same denominators.

The easiest way to do this is to multiply the denominators: For 2/5 + 1/2 multiply 5 by 2. Now you have a denominator of 10.

But now you have to change the top numbers too. Since you multiplied the 5 in 2/5 by 2, you also multiply the 2 by 2, to get 4. So the first fraction is now 4/10.

In the second fraction, you multiplied the denominator by 5, you have to multiply the numerator by 5 also, to get 5/10.

Now you have 4/10 + 5/10 and you can add 5 and 4 to get 9/10.

Simplest Form

To reduce a fraction to its simplest form, you have to arrange the numerator and denominator so the only common factor is 1.

Think of it this way:

Let's take an example: The fraction 2/10.

This is not reduced to its simplest terms because there is a number that will divide evenly into both: 2. We want to make it so that the only number that will divide evenly into both is 1.

Divide the top and bottom by 2 to get the new, reduced fraction - 1/5.

Multiplying Fractions

This is the easiest of all: Just multiply the two top numbers and then multiply the two bottom numbers.

Here is an example,

2/5 X 2/3

First, multiply the numerators: 2 X 2 = 4

then multiply the denominators: 5 X 3 = 15

Your answer is 4/15.

Dividing Fractions

Dividing fractions is easy if you remember a simple trick - first turn the second fraction upside down - then multiply!

Here is an example:

7/8 X 1/2

Turn the second fraction upside down:

7/8 X 2/1

then multiply:

(7 X 2) / (8 X 1) = 14/8

CONVERTING FRACTIONS TO DECIMALS

There are a couple of ways to convert fractions to decimals. The first, which is the fastest -- is to memorize some basic fraction facts.

1/100 is "one hundredth," expressed as a decimal, it's .01.

1/50 is "two hundredths," expressed as a decimal, it's .02.

1/25 is "one twenty-fifth" or "four hundredths," expressed as a decimal, it's .04.

1/20 is "one twentieth" or ""five hundredths," expressed as a decimal, it's .05.

1/10 is "one tenth," expressed as a decimal, it's .1.

1/8 is "one eighth," or "one hundred twenty-five thousandths," expressed as a decimal, it's .125.

1/5 is "one fifth," or "two tenths," expressed as a decimal, it's .2.

Analytical Thinking Inventory

1/4 is "one fourth" or "twenty-five hundredths," expressed as a decimal, it's .25.

1/3 is "one third" or "thirty-three hundredths," expressed as a decimal, it's .33.

1/2 is "one half" or "five tenths," expressed as a decimal, it's .5.

3/4 is "three fourths," or "seventy-five hundredths," expressed as a decimal, it's .75.

Of course, if you're no good at memorization, another good technique for converting a fraction to a decimal is to manipulate it so that the fraction's denominator is 10, 100, 1000, or some other power of 10.

Here's an example: We'll start with three quarters. What is the first number in the 4 "times table" that you can multiply and get a multiple of 10? Can you multiply 4 by something to get 10? No. Can you multiply it by something to get 100? Yes! 4 X 25 is 100.

So multiply the numerator by 25, which is 75 over 100

We know fractions are really a division problem, and we also know that dividing by 100, means we move the decimal 2 places to the left.

So, 75 over 100 = .75

Lets try another example - Convert one fifth to a decimal.

First find a power of 10 that 5 goes into evenly, which is 2.

Multiply the numerator and denominator by 2, which is two tenths.

Dividing 2 by 10 means we move the decimal place 1 place to the left.

So one fifth = zero point two

Converting Fractions to Percent

Working with fractions or percents can be intimidating enough. But converting from one to the other? That's a genuine nightmare for those who are not math wizards. But really, it doesn't have to be that way. Here are two ways to make it easier and faster to convert a fraction to a percent.

- First, you might remember that a fraction is nothing more than a division problem: you're dividing the bottom number into the top number. So for instance, if we start with a fraction 1/10, we are making a division problem with the 10 on the outside the bracket and the 1 on the inside. As you remember from your lessons on dividing by decimals, since 10 won't go into 1, you add a decimal and make it 10 into 1.0. 10 into 10 goes 1 time, and since it's behind the decimal, it's .1. And how do we say .1? We say "one tenth," which is exactly what we started with: 1/10. So we have a number we can work with now: .1. When we're dealing with percents, though, we're dealing strictly with hundredths (not tenths). You remember from studying decimals that adding a zero to the right of the number on the right side of the decimal does not change the value. Therefore, we can change .1 into .10 and have the same number--except now it's expressed as hundredths. We have 10 hundredths. That's ten out of 100--which is just another way of saying ten percent (ten per hundred or ten out of 100). In other words .1 = .10 = 10 percent. Remember, if you're changing from a decimal to a percent, get rid of the decimal on the left and replace it with a percent mark on the right: 10%. Let's review those steps again: Divide 10 into 1. Since 10 doesn't go into 1, turn 1 into 1.0. Now divide 10 into 1.0. Since 10 goes into 10 1 time, put it there and add your decimal to make it .1. Since a percent is always "hundredths," let's change .1 into .10. Then remove the decimal on the left and replace with a percent sign on the right. The answer is 10%.

- If you're doing these conversions on a multiple-choice test, here's an idea that might be even easier and faster. Let's say you have a fraction of 1/8 and you're asked what the percent is. Since we know that "percent" means hundredths, ask yourself what number we can multiply 8 by to get 100. Since there is no number, ask what number gets us close to 100. That number is 12: 8 X 12 = 96. So it gets us a little less than 100. Now, whatever you do to the denominator, you have to do to the numerator. Let's multiply 1 X 12 and we get 12. However, since 96 is a little less than 100, we know that our answer will be a percent a little MORE than 12%. So if your possible answers on the multiple-choice test are these:

a) 8.5%   b) 19%   c) 12.5%   d) 25%

then we know the answer is c) 12.5%, because it's a little MORE than the 12 we got in our math problem above.

Another way to look at this, using multiple choice strategy is you know the answer will be "about" 12. Looking at the other choices, they are all either too large or too small and can be eliminated right away.

This was an easy example to demonstrate, so don't be fooled! You probably won't get such an easy question on your exam, but the principle holds just the same. By estimating your answer quickly, you can eliminate choices immediately and save precious exam time.

Decimal Tips, Tricks and Shortcuts

Converting Decimals to Fractions

Converting decimals to fractions is easy if you say it the right way! If you say "point one" or "point 25", you'll have trouble.

But if you say, "one tenth" and "twenty-five hundredths," then you have already solved it! That's because, if you know your fractions, you know that "one tenth" looks like this: 1/10. And "twenty-five hundredths" looks like this: 25/100.

Even if you have digits before the decimal, such as 3.4, learning how to say the word will help you with the conversion into a fraction. It's not "three point four," it's "three and four tenths." Knowing this, you know that the fraction which looks like "three and four tenths" is 3 4/10.

The conversion is not complete until you reduce the fraction to its lowest terms: It's not 25/100, but 1/4.

Converting Decimals to Percent

Changing a decimal to a percent is easy if you remember one thing: multiply by 100.

For example, if you start with .45, simply multiply it by 100 for 45. Then add the % sign to the end - 45%.

Think of it this way: take out the decimal point, add a percent sign on the opposite side. In other words, the decimal on the left is replaced by the % on the right.

It doesn't work quite that easily if the decimal is in the middle of the number. For example, 3.7. Here, take out the decimal in the middle and replace it with a 0 % at the end. So 3.7 converted to decimal is 370%.

Percent Tips, Tricks and Shortcuts

Percent problems are not nearly as scary as they appear, if you remember this neat trick:

Draw a cross as in:

```
          |
  Portion | Percent
   _____|_____
          |
   Whole  | 100
          |
```

In the upper left, write PORTION. In the bottom left, write WHOLE. In the top right, write PERCENT and in the bottom right, write 100. Whatever your problem is, you will leave blank the unknown, and fill in the other four parts. For example, let's suppose your problem is: Find 10% of 50. Since we know the 10% part, we put 10 in the percent corner. Since the whole number in our problem is 50, we put that in the corner marked whole. You always put 100 underneath the percent, which leaves only the top left corner blank. This is where we'll put our answer - (usually X).

Now multiply the two corner numbers that are NOT 100. Here, it's 10 X 50 = 500. Now divide this by the remaining corner, or 100, to get a final answer of 5. 5 is the number that goes in the upper-left corner, and is your final solution. Another hint to remember: Percents are the same thing as hundredths in decimals. So .45 is the same as 45 hundredths or 45 percent.

Converting Percents to Decimals

Percents are a type of decimal, so it should be no surprise that converting between the two is actually fairly simple. Here are a few tricks and shortcuts to keep in mind:

- Remember that percent literally means "per 100" or "for every 100." So when you speak of 30% you're saying 30 for every 100 or the fraction 30/100. In basic math, you learned that fractions that have 10 or 100 as the denominator can easily be turned to a decimal. 30/100 is thirty hundredths, or expressed as a decimal, .30.
- Another way to look at it: To convert a percent to a decimal, simply divide the number by 100. So for instance, if the percent is 47%, divide 47 by 100. The result will be .47. Get rid of the % mark and you're done.
- Remember that the easiest way of dividing by 100 is by moving your decimal two spots to the left.

Converting Percents to Fractions

Converting percents to fractions is easy. After all, a percent is just a type of fraction; it tells you what part of 100 that you're talking about. Here are some simple ideas for making the conversion from a percent to a fraction:

- If the percent is a whole number -- say 34% -- then simply write a fraction with 100 as the denominator (the bottom number). Then put the percentage itself on top. So 34% becomes 34/100.
- Now reduce as you would reduce any percent. Here, by dividing 2 into 34 and 2 into 100, you get 17/50.
- If your percent is not a whole number -- say 3.4% --then convert it to a decimal expressed as hundredths. 3.4 is the same as 3.40 (or 3 and forty hundredths). Now ask yourself how you would express "three and forty hundredths" as a fraction. It would, of course, be 3 40/100. Reduce this and it becomes 3 2/5.

How to Answer Basic Math Multiple Choice

The time allowed on the math portion of a standardized test is typically so short that there's no room for error. You have to be fast and accurate.

Math strategy is very helpful, but nothing beats knowing your stuff! Make sure that you have learned all the important formulas that will be used.
If you don't know the formulas, strategy won't help you.

How to Answer Basic Math Questions - The Basics

First, read the problem, but not the answers.

Work through the problem first and come up with your own answers. Hopefully, you should find your answer among the choices.

If no answer matches the one you got, re-check your math, but this time, use a different method. In math, there are different ways to solve a problem.

Math Multiple Choice Strategy

The two strategies for working with basic math multiple choice are Estimation and Elimination.

Estimation is just as it sounds - try to estimate an approximate answer first. Then look at the choices.

Elimination is probably the most powerful strategy for answering multiple choice.

Eliminate obviously incorrect answers and narrowing the possible choices.

Here are a few basic math examples of how this works.

Solve 2/3 + 5/12

  a. 9/17
  b. 3/11
  c. 7/12
  d. 1 1/12

First estimate the answer. 2/3 is more than half and 5/12 is about half, so the answer is going to be very close to 1.

Next, Eliminate. Choice A is about 1/2 and can be eliminated, choice B is very small, less than 1/2 and can be eliminated. Choice C is close to 1/2 and can be eliminated. Leaving only choice D, which is just over 1.

Work through the solution, find a common denominator and add. The correct answer is 1 1/12, so Choice D is correct.

Let's look at another example:

Solve 4/5 – 2/3

  a. 2/2
  b. 2/13
  c. 1
  d. 2/15

First, quickly estimate the answer. 4/5 is very close to 1, and 2/3 more than half, so the answer is going to be less than 1/2.

Choice A can be eliminated right away, because it is 1. Choice C can be eliminated for the same reason.

Next, look at the denominators. Since 5 and 3 don't go into 13, choice B can be eliminated as well.

That leaves choice D. Checking the answer, the common

denominator will be 15. So the answer is 2/15 and choice D is correct.

Fractions shortcuts - Cancelling out

This is a powerful shortcut that saves you time and simplifies the problem into more manageable numbers!

If the numerator of one fractions has a common multiple with the denominator of the other fraction, you can cancel out.

Solve 2/15 ÷ 4/5

    a. 6/65
    b. 6/75
    c. 5/12
    d. 1/6

To divide fractions, multiply the first fraction with the inverse of the second.

So that gives 2/15 x 5/4. The numerator of the first fraction, 2, shares a multiple with the denominator of the second fraction, 4, which is 2. These cancel out, which gives,

1/15 X 5/2

We can cancel out again, since 15 and 5 are multiples, which gives,

1/3 x 1/2 = 1/6

Cancelling out solved the questions very quickly, but we can still use multiple choice strategies to answer.

Choice B can be eliminated because 75 is too large a denominator. Choice C can be eliminated because 5 and 15 don't go into 12.

Choice D is correct.

Decimal Multiple Choice Strategy and Shortcuts

Multiplying decimals gives a very quick way to estimate and eliminate choices. Anytime that you multiply decimals, it is going to give a answer with the same number of decimal places as the combined operands.

So for example,

2.38 X 1.2 will produce a number with three places of decimal, which is 2.856.
Here are a few examples with step-by-step explanation:
Solve 2.06 x 1.2

    a. 24.82

    b. 2.482

    c. 24.72

    d. 2.472

This is a simple question, but even before you start calculating, you can eliminate several choices. When multiplying decimals, there will always be as many numbers behind the decimal place in the answer as the sum of the ones in the initial problem, so Choices A and C can be eliminated.

The correct answer is D: 2.06 x 1.2 = 2.472

Solve 20.0 ÷ 2.5

    a. 12.05

    b. 9.25

    c. 8.3

    d. 8

First estimate the answer to be around 10, and eliminate Choice A. And since it'd also be an even number, you can eliminate Choice B and C., leaving only choice D.

The correct Answer is D: 20.0 ÷ 2.5 = 8

Part III - Quantitative Reasoning
Section II - Problem Solving

	A	B	C	D
1	○	○	○	○
2	○	○	○	○
3	○	○	○	○
4	○	○	○	○
5	○	○	○	○
6	○	○	○	○
7	○	○	○	○
8	○	○	○	○
9	○	○	○	○
10	○	○	○	○

1. Consider the following population growth chart.

Country	Population 2000	Population 2005
Japan	122,251,000	128,057,000
China	1,145,195,000	1,341,335,000
United States	253,339,000	310,384,000
Indonesia	184,346,000	239,871,000

What country is growing the fastest?

   a. Japan
   b. China
   c. United States
   d. Indonesia

2. A motorcycle is traveling at 100 km/hr. How far will it travel in 2 minutes?

   a. 1.6
   b. 3.3
   c. 1
   d. 12.5

3. Bill invests $4,000 at 8% compounded yearly. How much will he have in 2 years?

   a. $4320.00
   b. $4665.60
   c. $4640.00
   d. $4800.00

4. A waitress serves 10 tables one evening on her shift from 6 - 12:00 PM. She makes $10.50 per hour plus tips. Her total bills come to $240.60 with an average tip of 12%. How much did she make?

    a. 28.87
    b. $63.00
    c. $91.87
    d. $81.87

5. A man buys an item for $420 and has a balance of $3000.00. How much did he have before?

    a. $2,580
    b. $3,420
    c. $2,420
    d. $342

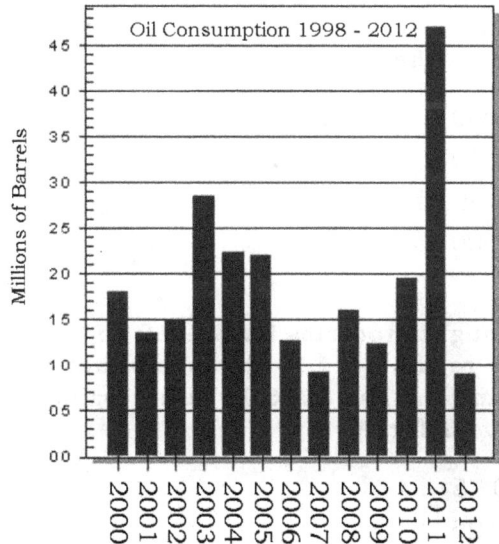

6. The graph above shows oil consumption in millions of barrels for the period, 1998 - 2012. What year did oil consumption peak?

    a. 2011
    b. 2010
    c. 2008
    d. 2009

7. 3 brothers eat a cake in the fridge. Henri eats 1/4 of the cake and Peter eats 2/5. How much is left for Brian?

    a. 7/20
    b. 3/5
    c. 3/4
    d. 9/20

8. A building is 40 feet long, 60 feet high and 20 feet deep. What is the volume?

    a. 40,000 cubic feet
    b. 48,000 square feet
    c. 48,000 cubic feet
    d. 40,000 square feet

9. Susan bought groceries for $29.50 and then met her friend, who repaid her $75 that she borrowed. When Susan got home she had $225.75 in her wallet. How much did she have before?

    a. 150.75
    b. 180.25
    c. 200.75
    d. 201.25

10. A person earns $25,000 per month and pays $9,000 income tax per year. The Government increased income tax by 0.5% per month and his monthly earning was increased $11,000. How much more income tax will he pay per month?

    a. $1260
    b. $1050
    c. $750
    d. $510

Answer Key

1. D
Indonesia is growing the fastest at about 30%.

2. B
First calculate the distance traveled in 1 minute.
100 km/hr. = 100/60 = 1.666 km/minute.
So, in 2 minutes the motorcycle will travel 3.33 kilometers.

3. B
For the first year, $4,000 invested at 8% will be 4000 X .08 = 320. The interest is compounded yearly, so to calculate the second years interest, 4320 X .08 = 345.60.
The total will then be 4320 + 345.60 = $4665.60

4. C
First calculate her hourly wage. 6 hours X 10.50/hour = $63. Next calculate tips. $240.60 X .12 = $28.87. So her total earnings will be 63 + 240.60 = $91.87

5. B
(Amount Spent) $420 + $3000 (Balance) = $3420

6. A
According to the graph, oil consumption peaked in 2011.

7. A
Setup the equation. 1/4 + 2/5 + X = 1
Find common denominator (20) so, 5/20 + 8/20 = 13/20.
So, 13/20 + X = 1.

X = 1 - 13/20
X = 7/20

8. B
The formula for a rectangular solid is Width X Depth X Height - so, 40 X 60 X 20 = 48,000 cubic feet.

9. B
First setup the equation. Let the total before equal X.
(X - 29.50) + 75 = 225.75

X - 29.50 = 225.75 - 75
X - 29.50 = 150.75
X = 150.75 + 29.50
X = 180.25

10. D

The income tax per year is $9,000. So, the income tax per month is 9,000/12 = $750.

This person earns $25,000 per month and pays $750 income tax. We need to find the rate of the income tax:
Tax rate: 750 * 100/25,000 = 3%

The Government increased this rate by 0.5% so it became 3.5%.

The income per month increased $11,000 so it became: $25,000 + $11,000 = $36,000.

The new monthly income tax is: 36,000•3.5/100 = $1260.

The amount of increase in tax per month is: $1260 - $750 = $510.

How to Solve Word Problems

Do you know what the biggest tip for solving word problems is?

Practice regularly and systematically.

Sounds simple and easy right? Yes it is, and yes it really does work.

Word problems are a way of thinking and require you to translate a real-world problem into mathematical terms.

Some math teachers say that learning how to think mathematically is the main reason for teaching word problems.

So what does that mean?

Studying word problems and math in general requires a logical and mathematical frame of mind. The only way you can get this is by practicing regularly, which means every day.

It is critical that you practice word problems every day for the 5 days before the exam as the absolute minimum.

If you practice and miss a day, you have lost the mathematical frame of mind and the benefit of your previous practice is gone. You must start all over again.

Everything is important.

All the information given in the problem has some purpose. There is no unnecessary information! Word problems are typically around 50 words in 2 or 3 sentences.

Often, the relationships are complicated. To explain everything, every word counts.

Make sure that you use every piece of information.

7 steps to solving word problems.

Step 1 – Read through the problem at least three times. The first reading should be a quick scan, and the next two readings should be done slowly to find answers to these questions:

> What does the problem ask? (Usually located at the end)

Mark all information and underline all important words or phrases.

Step 2 – Draw a picture. Use arrows, circles, lines, whatever works for you. This makes the problem real.

A favorite word problem is something like, 1 train leaves Station A travelling at 100 km/hr and another train leaves Station B travelling at 60 km/hr. ...

Draw a line, the two stations, and the two trains at either end.

Depending on the question, make a table with a blank portion to show information you don't know.

Step 3 — Assign a single letter to represent each unknown.

You may want to note the unknown that each letter represents so you don't get confused.

Step 4 – Translate the information into an equation.

Remember that the main problem with word problems is that they are not expressed in regular math equations. Your ability to identify correctly the variables and translate the information into an equation determines your ability to solve the problem.

Step 5 – Check the equation to see if it looks like regular equations that you are used to seeing and whether it looks sensible.

Does the equation appear to represent the information in the question? Take note that you may need to rewrite some formulas needed to solve the word problem equation.

Step 6 – Use algebra rules to solve the equation.

Simplify each side of the equation by removing parentheses and combining like terms.

Use addition or subtraction to isolate the variable term on one side of the equation. If a number crosses to the other side of the equation, the sign changes to the opposite -- for example positive to negative.

Use multiplication or division to solve for the variable. What you to once side of the equation you must do for the other.

Where there are multiple unknowns you will need to use elimination or substitution methods to resolve all the equations.

Step 7 – Check your final answers to see if they make sense with the information given in the problem.

For example, if the word problem involves a discount, the final price should be less or if a product was taxed then the final answer has to cost more.

TYPES OF WORD PROBLEMS

Word problems can be classified into 12 types. Below are examples of each type with a complete solution. Some types of word problems can be solved quickly using multiple choice strategies and some cannot. Always look for ways to estimate the answer and then eliminate choices.

1. Distance or speed

Two boats travel down a river towards the same destination, starting at the same time. One boat is traveling at 52 km/hr, and the other boat at 43 km/hr. How far apart will they be after 40 minutes?

    a. 46.67 km
    b. 19.23 km
    c. 6.04 km
    d. 14.39 km

Solution: C

After 40 minutes, the first boat will have traveled = 52 km/hr x 40 minutes/60 minutes = 34.7 km
After 40 minutes, the second boat will have traveled = 43 km/hr x 40/60 minutes = 28.66 km
Difference between the two boats will be 34.7 km – 28.66 km = 6.04 km.

Multiple Choice Strategy

First estimate the answer. The first boat is traveling 9 km. faster than the second, for 40 minutes, which is 2/3 of an hour. 2/3 of 9 = 6, as a rough guess of the distance apart.

Choices A, B and D can be eliminated right away.

2. Ratio

The instructions in a cookbook state that 700 grams of flour must be mixed in 100 ml of water, and 0.90 grams of salt added. A cook however has just 325 grams of flour. What is the quantity of water and salt that he should use?

    a. 0.41 grams and 46.4 ml
    b. 0.45 grams and 49.3 ml
    c. 0.39 grams and 39.8 ml
    d. 0.25 grams and 40.1 ml

Solution: A

The Cookbook states 700 grams of flour, but the cook only has 325. The first step is to determine the percentage of flour he has 325/700 x 100 = 46.4%
That means that 46.4% of all other items must also be used.
46.4% of 100 = 46.4 ml of water
46.4% of 0.90 = 0.41 grams of salt.

Multiple Choice Strategy

The recipe calls for 700 grams of flour but the cook only has 325, which is just less than half, the quantity of water and salt are going to be about half.

Choices C and D can be eliminated right away. Choice B is very close so be careful. Looking closely at choice B, it is exactly half, and since 325 is slightly less than half of 700, it can't be correct.
Choice A is correct.

3. Percent

An agent received $6,685 as his commission for selling a property. If his commission was 13% of the selling price, how much was the property?

    a. $68,825
    b. $121,850
    c. $49,025
    d. $51,423

Solution: D

Let's assume that the property price is x
That means from the information given, 13% of x = 6,685

Solve for x,
x = 6685 x 100/13 = $51,423

Multiple Choice Strategy

The commission, 13%, is just over 10%, which is easier to work with. Round up $6685 to $6700, and multiple by 10 for an approximate answer. 10 X 6700 = $67,000. You can do this in your head. Choice B is much too big and can be eliminated. Choice C is too small and can be eliminated. Choices A and D are left and good possibilities.

Do the calculations to make the final choice.

4. Sales & Profit

A store owner buys merchandise for $21,045. He transports them for $3,905 and pays his staff $1,450 to stock the merchandise on his shelves. If he does not incur further costs, how much does he need to sell the items to make $5,000 profit?

    a. $32,500
    b. $29,350
    c. $32,400
    d. $31,400

Solution: D

Total cost of the items is $21,045 + $3,905 + $1,450 = $26,400
Total cost is now $26,400 + $5000 profit = $31,400

Multiple Choice Strategy

Round off and add the numbers up in your head quickly.
21,000 + 4,000 + 1500 = 26500. Add in 5000 profit for a total of 31500.

Choice B is too small and can be eliminated. Choice C and Choice A are too large and can be eliminated.

5. Tax/Income

A woman earns $42,000 per month and pays 5% tax on her monthly income. If the Government increases her monthly taxes by $1,500, what is her income after tax?

    a. $38,400
    b. $36,050
    c. $40,500
    d. $39, 500

Solution: A
Initial tax on income was 5/100 x 42,000 = $2,100
$1,500 was added to the tax to give $2,100 + 1,500 = $3,600
Income after tax is $42,000 - $3,600 = $38,400

6. Simple Interest

Simple interest is one type of interest problems. There are always four variables of any simple interest equation. With simple interest, you would be given three of these variables and be asked to solve for one unknown variable. With more complex interest problems, you would have to solve for multiple variables.

The four variables of simple interest are:
P – Principal which refers to the original amount of money put in the account
I – Interest or the amount of money earned as interest
r – Rate or interest rate. This MUST ALWAYS be in decimal format and not in percentage
t – Time or the amount of time the money is kept in the account to earn interest

The formula for simple interest is I = P x r x t

Example 1

A customer deposits $1,000 in a savings account with a bank that offers 2% interest. How much interest will be earned after 4 years?

For this problem, there are 3 variables as expected.

P = $1,000
t = 4 years
r = 2%
I = ?

Before we can begin solving for I using the simple interest formula, we need to first convert the rate from percentage to decimal.

2% = 2/100 = 0.02
Now we can use the formula: I = P x r x t

I = 1,000 x 0.02 x 4 = 80
This means that the $1,000 would have earned an interest of $80 after 4 years. The total in the account after 4 years will thus be principal + interest earned, or 1,000 + 80 = $1,080

Example 2

Sandra deposits $1400 in a savings account with a bank at 5% interest. How long will she have to leave the money in the bank to earn $420 as interest to buy a second-hand car?

In this example, the given information is:
I = $420
P = $1,400
r - 5%
t - ?
As usual, first we convert the rate from percentage to decimal
5% = 5/100 = 0.05

Next, we plug in the variables we know into the simple interest formula - I = P x r x t

420 = 1,400 x 0.05 x t
420 = 70 x t
420 = 70t
t = 420/70
t = 6

Sandra will have to leave her $1,400 in the bank for 6 years to earn her an interest of $420 at a rate of 5%.

Other important simple interest formula to remember

To use this formula below, do not convert r (rate) to decimal.

P = 100 x interest/ r x t
r = 100 x interest/p x t
t = 100 x interest/ p x r

7. Averaging

The average weight of 10 books is 54 grams. 2 more books were added and the average weight became 55.4. If one of the 2 new books added weighed 62.8 g, what is the weight of the other?

    a. 44.7 g
    b. 67.4 g
    c. 62 g
    d. 52 g

Solution: C

Total weight of 10 books with average 54 grams will be = 10 × 54 = 540 g
Total weight of 12 books with average 55.4 will be = 55.4 × 12 = 664.8 g
So total weight of the remaining 2 will be= 664.8 – 540 = 124.8 g
If one weighs 62.8, the weight of the other will be= 124.8 g – 62.8 g = 62 g

Multiple Choice Strategy

Averaging problems can be estimated by looking at which direction the average goes. If additional items are added and the average goes up, the new items much be greater than the average. If the average goes down after new items are added, the new items must be less than the average.

Here, the average is 54 grams and 2 books are added which increases the average to 55.4, so the new books must weight more than 54 grams.

Choices A and D can be eliminated right away.

8. Probability

A bag contains 15 marbles of various colors. If 3 marbles are white, 5 are red and the rest are black, what is the probability of randomly picking out a black marble from the bag?

    a. 7/15
    b. 3/15
    c. 1/5
    d. 4/15

Solution: A

Total marbles = 15
Number of black marbles = 15 – (3 + 5) = 7
Probability of picking out a black marble = 7/15

9. Geometry

The length of a rectangle is 5 in. more than its width. The perimeter of the rectangle is 26 in. What is the width and length of the rectangle?

    a. width = 6 inches, Length = 9 inches
    b. width = 4 inches, Length = 9 inches
    c. width = 4 inches, Length = 5 inches
    d. width = 6 inches, Length = 11 inches

Solution: B

Formula for perimeter of a rectangle is 2(L + W)
p=26, so 2(L+W) = p
The length is 5 inches more than the width, so
2(w+5) + 2w = 26
2w + 10 + 2w = 26
2w + 2w = 26 - 10
4w = 16

W = 16/4 = 4 inches

L is 5 inches more than w, so L = 5 + 4 = 9 inches.

10. Totals and fractions

A basket contains 125 oranges, mangos and apples. If 3/5 of the fruits in the basket are mangos and only 2/5 of the mangos are ripe, how many ripe mangos are there in the basket?

    a. 30
    b. 68
    c. 55
    d. 47

Solution: A
Number of mangos in the basket is 3/5 x 125 = 75
Number of ripe mangos = 2/5 x 75 = 30

CALCULATING PERIMETER, AREA AND VOLUME

	Circle	Triangle	Square	Rectangle
Perimeter	$2\prod r$	a + b + c	4a	2(H + w)
Area	$\prod r^2$	1/2bh	2a	lw

Written Communication Summary WCT

THIS SECTION CONTAINS A SELF-ASSESSMENT AND TUTORIALS. The tutorials are designed to familiarize general principles and the self-assessment contains general questions similar to the WCT questions likely to be on the Police Constable exam, but are not intended to be identical. The tutorials are not designed to be a complete course, and it is assumed that students have some familiarity with this type of material. If you do not understand parts of the tutorials, or find the tutorials difficult, it is recommended that you seek out additional instruction.

Tour of the WCT Content

Below is a detailed list of the types of reading questions that generally appear on your exam.

- Drawing logical conclusions (Syllogisms)
- Summarizing
- Ordering information
- Distinguishing important facts from details

The questions below are not the same as you will find on the exam - that would be too easy! And nobody knows what the questions will be and they change all the time. Mostly the changes consist of substituting new questions for old, but the changes can be new question formats or styles, changes to the number of questions in each section, changes to the time limits for each section and combining sections. Below are general reading and vocabulary questions that cover the same areas as the exam. So the format and exact wording of the questions may differ slightly, and change from year to year, if you can answer the questions below, you will have no problem with the WCT section of the test.

WCT Self-Assessment

The purpose of the self-assessment is:

- Identify your strengths and weaknesses.
- Develop your personalized study plan (above)
- Get accustomed to the Police Constable test format
- Extra practice – the self-assessments are almost a full 3rd practice test!
- Provide a baseline score for preparing your study schedule.

Once complete, use the table below to assess your understanding of the content, and prepare your study schedule described in chapter 1.

80% - 100%	Excellent – you have mastered the content
60 – 79%	Good. You have a working knowledge. Even though you can just pass this section, you may want to review the tutorials and do some extra practice to see if you can improve your mark.
40% - 59%	Below Average. You do not understand reading comprehension problems. Review the tutorials , and retake this quiz again in a few days, before proceeding to the Practice Test Questions.
Less than 40%	Poor. You have a very limited understanding of reading comprehension problems. Please review the tutorials , and retake this quiz again in a few days, before proceeding to the Practice Test Questions.

Scenario: Traffic Accident

A police patrol car arrived the scene at 10.07AM. A blue SUV ran a red stop light at the intersection of Fort and Birch. Three smartly dressed teenage girls were standing in front of a restaurant, by the side of the intersection when the accident happened. The driver of the blue SUV was the owner of a shop that sold kiddies clothes and toys. It was a clear Sunday morning, two days before the start of the New Year. A brightly painted ice cream truck was coming some distance behind the yellow Honda before the accident. The Yellow Honda was driven by a woman with her two kids at the back. A man who witnessed the accident immediately called the police at 10.03AM. Fortunately, the driver of the SUV only had a slight cut in his head, while the woman and her kids were unhurt. There were pieces of broken glass on the road. The accident caused a major holdup as motorist had to slowdown. The paramedics arrived the scene at 10.10AM to attend to the accident victims. The blue SUV ran into a yellow Honda coming across the road from the right. The Honda was badly damaged at the back fender and the back windscreen was shattered. The SUV was heavily damaged in the front. The cars were cleared of the road and traffic restored by 10.15AM. The witness was on his way to the bank when he witnessed the accident.

SUGGESTED ANSWER

Here the facts are divided into categories, Description of the accident, Damage, Injuries, and Witnesses.

Description of the Accident and Chronology
A blue SUV ran a red stop light at the intersection of Fort and Birch. The blue SUV ran into a yellow Honda coming across the road from the right.

A man who witnessed the accident immediately called the police at 10.03AM.

A police patrol car arrived the scene at 10.07AM.

The paramedics arrived the scene at 10.10AM to attend to the accident victims.

The cars were cleared of the road and traffic restored by 10.15AM.

Damage
The Honda was badly damaged at the back fender and the back windscreen shattered. The SUV was heavily damaged in the front.

Injuries
The driver of the SUV had a slight cut in his head, while the woman and her kids were unhurt. The accident caused a major holdup as motorist had to slowdown.

Witnesses
3 teenage girls (possible)
Male witness on way to the bank

Details (Not included in Report)
Three smartly dressed teenage girls were standing in front of a restaurant, by the side of the intersection when the accident happened.

The driver of the blue SUV was the owner of a shop that sold kiddies clothes and toys.

It was a clear Sunday morning, two days before the start of the New Year.

A brightly painted ice cream truck was coming some distance behind the yellow Honda before the accident.

There were pieces of broken glass on the road.

The witness was on his way to the bank when he witnessed the accident.

The Yellow Honda was driven by a woman with her two kids at the back.

Main Idea and Supporting Details

Identifying the main idea, topic and supporting details in a passage can feel like an overwhelming task. The passages used for standardized tests can be boring and seem difficult - Test writers don't use interesting passages or ones that talk about things most people are familiar with. Despite these obstacles, all passages and paragraphs will have the information you need to answer the questions.

The topic of a passage or paragraph is its subject. It's the general idea and can be summed up in a word or short phrase. On some standardized tests, there is a short description of the passage if it's taken from a longer work. Make sure you read the description as it might state the topic of the passage. If not, read the passage and ask yourself, "Who or what is this about?" For example:

> Over the years, school uniforms have been hotly debated. Arguments are made that students have the right to show individuality and express themselves by choosing their own clothes. However, this brings up social and academic issues. Some kids cannot afford to wear the clothes they like and might be bul-

lied by the "better dressed" students. With attention drawn to clothes and the individual, students will lose focus on class work and the reason they are in school. School uniforms should be mandatory.

Ask: What is this paragraph about?

Topic: school uniforms

Once you have the topic, it's easier to find the main idea. The main idea is a specific statement telling what the writer wants you to know about the topic. Writers usually state the main idea as a thesis statement. If you're looking for the main idea of a single paragraph, the main idea is called the topic sentence and will probably be the first or last sentence. If you're looking for the main idea of an entire passage, look for the thesis statement in either the first or last paragraph. The main idea is usually restated in the conclusion. To find the main idea of a passage or paragraph, follow these steps:

1. Find the topic.

2. Ask yourself, "What point is the author trying to make about the topic?"

3. Create your own sentence summarizing the author's point.

4. Look in the text for the sentence closest in meaning to yours.

Look at the example paragraph again. It's already established that the topic of the paragraph is school uniforms. What is the main idea/topic sentence?

Ask: "What point is the author trying to make about school uniforms?"

Summary: Students should wear school uniforms.

Topic sentence: School uniforms should be mandatory.

Main Idea: School uniforms should be mandatory.

Each paragraph offers supporting details to explain the main idea. The details could be facts or reasons, but they will always answer a question about the main idea. What? Where? Why? When? How? How much/many? Look at the example paragraph again. You'll notice that more than one sentence answers a question about the main idea. These are the supporting details.

Main Idea: School uniforms should be mandatory.

Ask: Why? Some kids cannot afford to wear clothes they like and could be bullied by the "better dressed" kids. Supporting Detail

With attention drawn to clothes and the individual, Students will lose focus on class work and the reason they are in school. Supporting Detail

What if the author doesn't state the main idea in a topic sentence? The passage will have an implied main idea. It's not as difficult to find as it might seem. Paragraphs are always organized around ideas. To find an implied main idea, you need to know the topic and then find the relationship between the supporting details. Ask yourself, "What is the point the author is making about the relationship between the details?"

> Cocoa is what makes chocolate good for you. Chocolate comes in many varieties. These delectable flavors include milk chocolate, dark chocolate, semi-sweet, and white chocolate.

Ask: What is this paragraph about?

Topic: Chocolate

Ask: What? Where? Why? When? How? How much/many?

Supporting details: Chocolate is good for you because it is made of cocoa, Chocolate is delicious, Chocolate comes in different delicious flavors

Ask: What is the relationship between the details and what is the author's point?

Main Idea: Chocolate is good because it is healthy and it tastes good.

PRACTICE TEST QUESTIONS SET 1

The questions below are not the same as you will find on the Ontario Police Exam - that would be too easy! And nobody knows what the questions will be and they change all the time. Below are general questions that cover the same subject areas as the exam. So, while the format and exact wording of the questions may differ slightly, and change from year to year, if you can answer the questions below, you will have no problem with the exam.

For the best results, take these Practice Test Questions as if it were the real exam. Set aside time when you will not be disturbed, and a location that is quiet and free of distractions. Read the instructions carefully, read each question carefully, and answer to the best of your ability.
Use the bubble answer sheets provided. When you have completed the Practice Questions, check your answer against the Answer Key and read the explanation provided.

Do not attempt more than one set of practice test questions in one day. After completing the first practice test, wait two or three days before attempting the second set of questions.

Police Analytical Thinking Inventory PATI

Part I - Deductive Reasoning

    Syllogisms - 15 Questions

    Mapping - 15 Questions

Part II - Inductive Reasoning

    Matching - 15 questions

    Sequences - 15 questions

Part III Quantitative Reasoning

    Basic Math - 15 questions

    Problem Solving - 15 Questions

Written Communication Test WCT

1 question

Syllogism Answer Sheet

	A	B	C	D
1	○	○	○	○
2	○	○	○	○
3	○	○	○	○
4	○	○	○	○
5	○	○	○	○
6	○	○	○	○
7	○	○	○	○
8	○	○	○	○
9	○	○	○	○
10	○	○	○	○
11	○	○	○	○
12	○	○	○	○
13	○	○	○	○
14	○	○	○	○
15	○	○	○	○

Mapping Answer Sheet

	A	B	C	D
1	○	○	○	○
2	○	○	○	○
3	○	○	○	○
4	○	○	○	○
5	○	○	○	○
6	○	○	○	○
7	○	○	○	○
8	○	○	○	○
9	○	○	○	○
10	○	○	○	○
11	○	○	○	○
12	○	○	○	○
13	○	○	○	○
14	○	○	○	○
15	○	○	○	○

Matching Answer Sheet

	A	B	C	D
1	○	○	○	○
2	○	○	○	○
3	○	○	○	○
4	○	○	○	○
5	○	○	○	○
6	○	○	○	○
7	○	○	○	○
8	○	○	○	○
9	○	○	○	○
10	○	○	○	○
11	○	○	○	○
12	○	○	○	○
13	○	○	○	○
14	○	○	○	○
15	○	○	○	○

Sequences Answer Sheet

	A	B	C	D
1	○	○	○	○
2	○	○	○	○
3	○	○	○	○
4	○	○	○	○
5	○	○	○	○
6	○	○	○	○
7	○	○	○	○
8	○	○	○	○
9	○	○	○	○
10	○	○	○	○
11	○	○	○	○
12	○	○	○	○
13	○	○	○	○
14	○	○	○	○
15	○	○	○	○

Basic Math Answer Sheet

	A	B	C	D
1	○	○	○	○
2	○	○	○	○
3	○	○	○	○
4	○	○	○	○
5	○	○	○	○
6	○	○	○	○
7	○	○	○	○
8	○	○	○	○
9	○	○	○	○
10	○	○	○	○
11	○	○	○	○
12	○	○	○	○
13	○	○	○	○
14	○	○	○	○
15	○	○	○	○

Problem Solving Answer Sheet

	A	B	C	D
1	○	○	○	○
2	○	○	○	○
3	○	○	○	○
4	○	○	○	○
5	○	○	○	○
6	○	○	○	○
7	○	○	○	○
8	○	○	○	○
9	○	○	○	○
10	○	○	○	○
11	○	○	○	○
12	○	○	○	○
13	○	○	○	○
14	○	○	○	○
15	○	○	○	○

Police Analytical Thinking Inventory (PATI)

Part I - Deductive Reasoning
Section I - Syllogisms

6. Some cats have no tails. All cats are mammals. Some mammals have no tails.

If the first 2 statements are true, then the third statement is:

   a. True
   b. False
   c. Uncertain

2. All students carry backpacks. My grandfather carries a backpack. Therefore, my grandfather is a student.

If the first 2 statements are true, then the third statement is:

   a. True
   b. False
   c. Uncertain

3. All dogs are mammals. No cats are dogs. Therefore, no cats are mammals.

If the first 2 statements are true, then the third statement is:

   a. True
   b. False
   c. Uncertain

4. All cats are felines. All cats are mammals. All mammals are felines.

If the first 2 statements are true, then the third statement is:

   a. True
   b. False
   c. Uncertain

5. No mammals are fish. Some fish are not whales. Some whales are not mammals.

If the first 2 statements are true, then the third statement is:

   a. True
   b. False
   c. Uncertain

6. No fish are dogs, and no dogs can fly. All fish can fly.

If the first 2 statements are true, then the third statement is:

   a. True
   b. False
   c. Uncertain

7. All colonels are officers. All officers are soldiers. No colonels are soldiers.

If the first 2 statements are true, then the third statement is:

   a. True
   b. False
   c. Uncertain

8. Krizzia loves reading books. Nea enjoys playing with her dolls. Krizzia and Nea are cousins.

    a. Krizzia likes to play with Nea.

    b. Nea finds reading boring.

    c. Krizzia and Nea are blood related

    d. Nea and Krizzia are best friends.

9. The village is found in a coastal area. Many fishermen go out to sea everyday. They go home late in the afternoon.

    a. Fishing is the means of living of the villagers.

    b. Many fishermen hate fishing.

    c. Fishermen go out to sea especially in the evening.

    d. The village attracts tourists.

10. Ben and Ted are classmates. They would ride the school bus together. They also have lunch at the same table. They're even lab partners.

    a. Ben and Ted don't like each other.

    b. Ben prefers being with other children.

    c. Ben and Ted are inseparable.

    d. Ted is always alone.

11. Karen takes care of her garden everyday. She grows fruits and vegetables. She always waters them. She also pulls out the weeds and put fertilizer on her plants.

    a. Karen hates taking care of her plants.

    b. Karen is fond of gardening.

    c. Karen plants flowers in her garden.

    d. Karen and her mother work on the garden together.

PRACTICE TEST QUESTIONS 1

12. Collecting stamps is Tom's hobby. He started collecting stamps when he was six years old. Today, Tom has over a thousand stamps in his collection.

    a. Tom collects stamp albums.

    b. Tom started collecting stamps in high school.

    c. Tom is a stamp collector.

    d. Collecting stamps is an expensive hobby.

13. Mother went to market. She bought apples, oranges, and bananas. She also bought cabbage, beans, and squash.

    a. Vegetables in the market are expensive.

    b. Mother bought chicken and meat.

    c. Many people went to the market.

    d. Mother bought fruits and vegetables.

14. Tommy and Timmy are brothers. They look the same. They also have the same birthdays.

    a. Tommy is older than Timmy.

    b. Timmy is more handsome than Tommy.

    c. Tommy and Timmy are twins.

    d. Tommy and Timmy are best friends.

15. Girls love roses. They smell so sweet. Their colors are also very attractive.

    a. Roses are fragrant.

    b. Roses attract bees.

    c. Boys love roses.

    d. Girls don't like roses.

Section II - Mapping

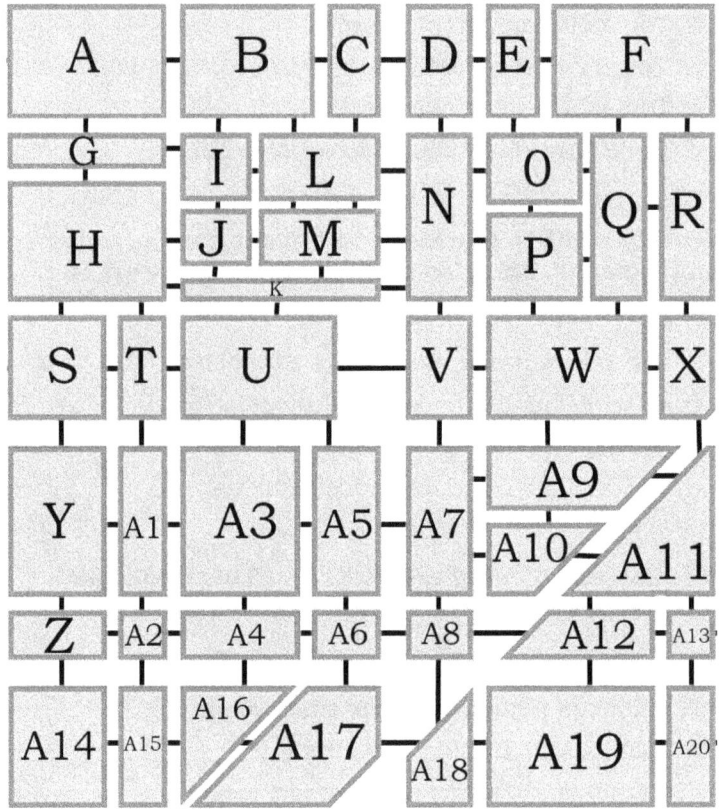

Map Key

Each Square labeled A to Z and A1 to A20 represent the corner of an intersection. The lines between the squares represent a city block. The intersections and city blocks fall into 3 categories.

Large blocks: A, B,F, H, N, Q, R, U, W, Y, A3, A5, A7, A9, A11, A14, A17, A19
Small blocks: C, D, E, I. J, L,M, O, P, S, T, V, X, A1, A4, A10, Z, A12, A15, A16, A18, A20

Mini blocks: G, K, A2, A6, A8, A13

The time it to travel between city block is:

Large blocks

In a car: 4 minutes
On a bike: 6 minutes
On foot: 10 minutes

Small Blocks

In a car: 3 minutes
On a bike: 5 minutes
On foot: 8 minutes

Mini Blocks

In a car: 2 minutes
On a bike: 4 minutes
On foot: 6 minutes

1. A car travels from block X to A6. What is the shortest possible time it would spend if it had to spend 2 minutes to buy gas?

    a. 15 minutes

    b. 12 minutes

    c. 17 minutes

    d. 14 minutes

2. How fast can you walk from block B to V without passing through blocks L and N?

    a. 52 minutes

    b. 42 minutes

    c. 45 minutes

    d. 38 minutes

3. A pizza delivery boy on bike in block A9 has to make a delivery in A20. What is the shortest time it would take him to get if he rides his bike the first 2 blocks and walks the rest of the way?

   a. 18 minutes
   b. 20 minutes
   c. 17 minutes
   d. 22 minutes

4. A car moves from block Y to block A17. Along the way it goes through block A2 and A5. What is the shortest time it could have taken if it is not allowed to go through the same block twice?

   a. 19 minutes
   b. 29 minutes
   c. 20 minutes
   d. 22 minutes

5. What is the shortest time it would take to bike from block H to block A4 if you must pass through block Y?

   a. 30 minutes
   b. 26 minutes
   c. 18 minutes
   d. 28 minutes

6. How fast can it take a police car to travel from block Z to V if it has to spend 15 seconds extra at each intersection it drives pass?

   a. 15 minutes 45 seconds
   b. 16 minutes 45 seconds
   c. 17 minutes
   d. 17 minutes 45 seconds

7. Which of the following would be the shortest?

Driving from block Z to A12
Walking from block A to D
Driving from A to C and then walking to D
Riding a bike from block T to A14

    a. driving from block z to a12
    b. walking from block a to d
    c. driving from a to c and then walking to d
    d. riding a bike from block t to a14

8. Which of these would take the most time?

Walking from A3 to K
Riding a bike from A3 to A10
Driving a car from A3 to S
Riding a bike from A3 to y, then driving a car to H

    a. walking from a3 to k
    b. riding a bike from a3 to a10
    c. driving a car from a3 to s
    d. riding a bike from a3 to y, then driving a car to h

9. If you had to spend 15 extra seconds at each intersection, how long would it take from block F to block V by bike, using the shortest route?

    a. 15 minutes
    b. 12 minutes
    c. 14 minutes
    d. 17 minutes

10. A driver needs to go from block F to V. How many possible route combinations can he use if he must pass through only 4 blocks between F and V?

    a. 5 routes
    b. 4 routes
    c. 3 routes
    d. 6 routes

11. A driver needs to drive from block F to V. What is the fastest time he can use if he must pass through only 4 blocks between F and V?

    a. 15 minutes
    b. 16 minutes
    c. 17 minutes
    d. 19 minutes

12. How fast would a bike rider move from block H to X?

    a. 24 minutes
    b. 27 minutes
    c. 25 minutes
    d. 26 minutes

13. How long would it take a man to move from block H to X if he drove a car the first 3 blocks and then rode a bike the rest of the way, using the fastest route?

    a. 18 minutes
    b. 21 minutes
    c. 22 minutes
    d. 20 minutes

14. **How long would it take to move from block D to A6, by car for the first block, by bike for the next 2 blocks and then on foot the rest of the way, using the fastest route?**

    a. 30 minutes
    b. 25 minutes
    c. 32 minutes
    d. 28 minutes

15. **How fast does it take by bike from block G to P with a one minute stop at each intersection?**

    a. 22 minutes
    b. 19 minutes
    c. 23 minutes
    d. 25 minutes

Part II - Inductive Reasoning

Section I - Matching

Directions: In each of the following questions, select the choice that does not belong with the other three.

1.

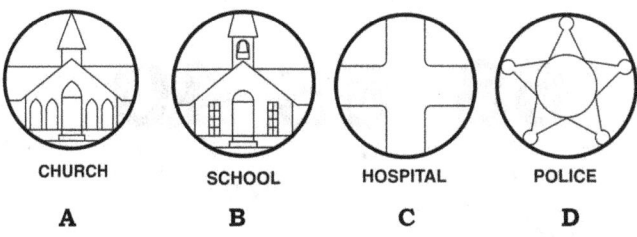

2.

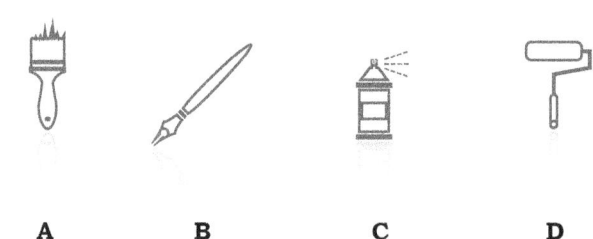

    A   B   C   D

3.

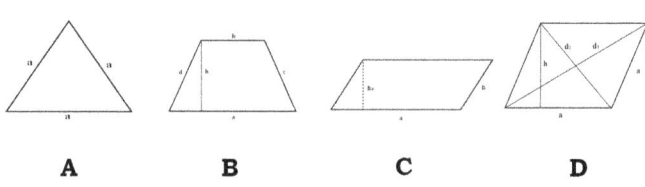

    A   B   C   D

4.

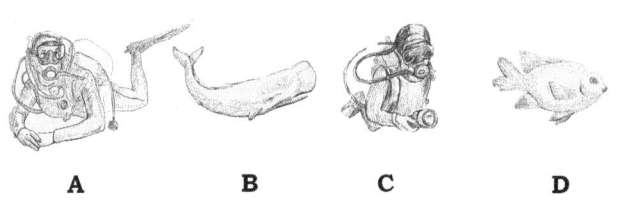

    A   B   C   D

5.

    A   B   C   D

6.

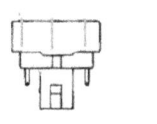 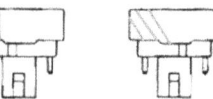 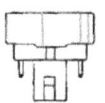

A   B   C   D

7.

A   B   C   D

8.

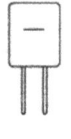 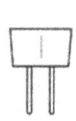 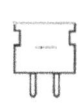 

A   B   C   D

9.

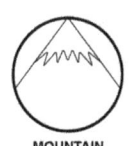   

MOUNTAIN   CURVE   DO NOT ENTER   NO PARKING

A   B   C   D

10.

   A   B   C   D

11.

31 37 41 46

 A   B   C   D

12.

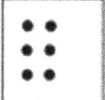 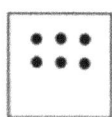 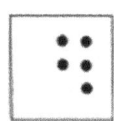 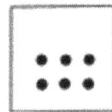

   A   B   C   D

13.

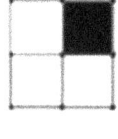 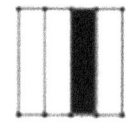 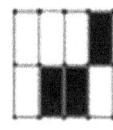 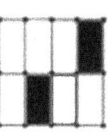

   A   B   C   D

14.

1/3   2/10   1/6   1/4
 A   B   C   D

15.

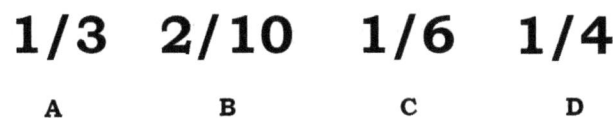

 A   B   C   D

Section II - Sequences

Directions: Complete the sequence from the choices given.

1.

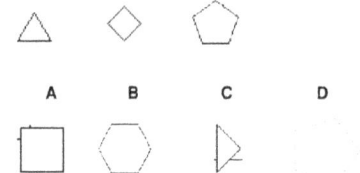

2.

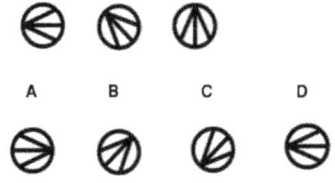

3.

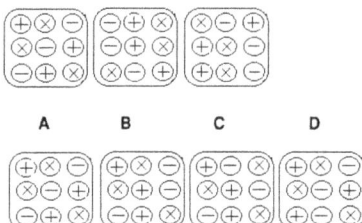

4.

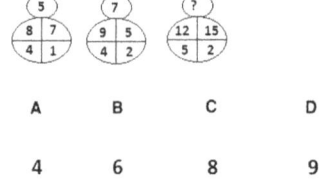

     A   B   C   D

     4   6   8   9

5.

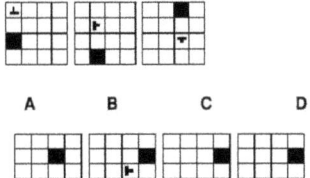

6.

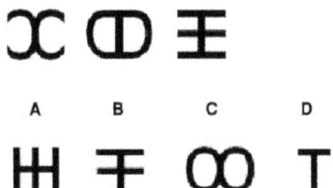

7.

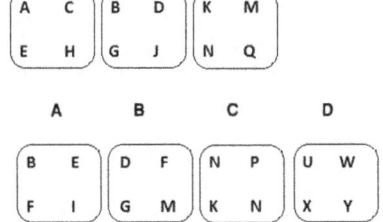

8.

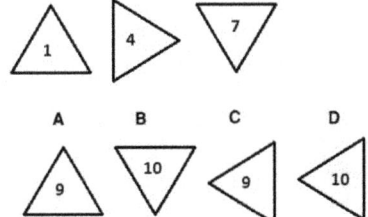

9.

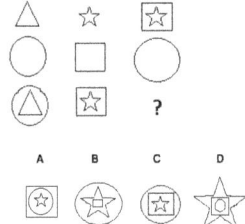

10.

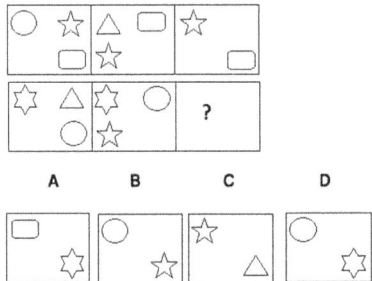

11.

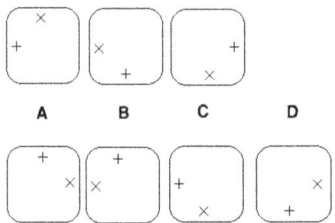

12.

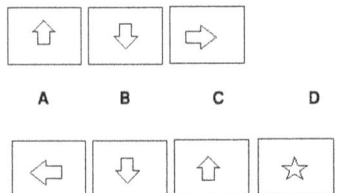

13.

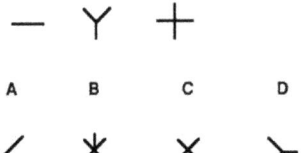

14.

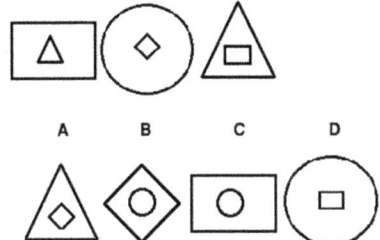

15.

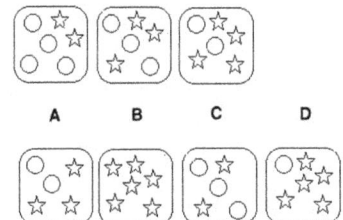

Part III Quantitative Reasoning
Basic Math

1. 1518 ÷ 27 =

    a. 54 r1
    b. 56 r6
    c. 55 r3
    d. 59 r2

2. 1628 / 4 =

    a. 307
    b. 667
    c. 447
    d. 407

3. 143 * 4 =

    a. 572
    b. 702
    c. 467
    d. 672

4. 7050 − 305 =

    a. 6705
    b. 6745
    c. 5745
    d. 6045

5. 305 * 25 =

    a. 6525
    b. 7625
    c. 5026
    d. 7026

6. 5x + 3 = 7x -1. Find x

    a. 1/3
    b. 1/2
    c. 1
    d. 2

7. 5x + 2(x + 7) = 14x – 7. Find x

    a. 1
    b. 2
    c. 3
    d. 4

8. 12t - 10 = 14t +2. Find t

    a. -6
    b. -4
    c. 4
    d. 6

9. 3/5 + 7/10

    a. 1/10
    b. 7/10
    c. 1 3/10
    d. 1 1/12

10. 7/15 – 3/10

    a. 1/6
    b. 4/5
    c. 1/7
    d. 1 1/3

11. 3.57 - 3.21

    a. 3.6
    b. 0.036
    c. 0.36
    d. 0.136

12. Convert 19% to decimal

    a. 0.0019
    b. 0.19
    c. 0.019
    d. 1.9

13. Convert 1.21 to percent

    a. 121%
    b. 12.1%
    c. 1.21%
    d. 0.121%

14. Convert 4.358 to percent

    a. 435.8%
    b. 43.58%
    c. 4.358%
    d. 4358%

15. 9.065 - 4.071

   A. 5.994
   B. 4.094
   C. 49.94
   D. 4.994

Section II - Problem Solving

1. A woman spent 15% of her income on an item and ends with $120. What percentage of her income is left?

   a. 12%
   b. 85%
   c. 75%
   d. 95%

2. A mother is making spaghetti for her son. The recipe that she's using says that for 500 grams of spaghetti, she should add 0.75 grams of salt. However, the mom just wants 125 grams of spaghetti. Based on this information, how much salt should she use?

   a. 0.38 grams
   b. 0.75 grams
   c. 0.19 grams
   d. 0.25 grams

3. A pet store sold $19,304.56 worth of merchandise in June. If the cost of products sold was $5,284.34, employees were paid $8,384.76, and rent was $2,920.00, how much profit did the store make in June?

    a. $5,635.46
    b. $2,714.46
    c. $14,020.22
    d. $10,019.80

4. At the beginning of 2009, Madalyn invested $5,000 in a savings account. The account pays 4% interest per year. At the end of the year, after the interest was awarded, how much did Madalyn have in the account?

    a. $5,200
    b. $5,020
    c. $5,110
    d. $7,000

5. If 144 students need to go on a trip and the buses each carry 36 students, how many buses are needed?

    a. 6
    b. 5
    c. 4
    d. 3

6. If a square if five feet tall, what is its area?

    a. 5 square feet
    b. 10 square feet
    c. 20 square feet
    d. 25 square feet

7. John is a barber and receives 40% of the amount paid by each of his customers. John gets all tips paid to him. If a man pays $8.50 for a haircut and pays a tip of $1.30, how much money goes to John?

   a. $3.92
   b. $4.70
   c. $5.30
   d. $6.40

8. Susan was surprised to find she had two more quarters than she believed she had in her purse. If quarters are the only coins, and the total is $8.75, how many quarters did she think she had?

   a. 35
   b. 29
   c. 31
   d. 33

9. There were some oranges in a basket, by adding 8/5 of these, the total became 130. How many oranges were in the basket?

   a. 60
   b. 50
   c. 40
   d. 35

10. Mr. Brown bought 5 burgers, 3 drinks, 4 fries for his family and a cookie for the dog. If the price of all single items is same, at $1.30 and a 3.5% tax is added, then what is the total cost of dinner?

    a. $16.00
    b. $16.90
    c. $17.00
    d. $17.50

11. A distributor purchased 550 kilograms of potatoes for $165. He distributed these at a rate of $6.4 per 20 kilograms to 15 shops, $3.4 per 10 kilograms to 12 shops and the remainder at $1.8 per 5 kilograms. If his total distribution cost is $10, what will his profit be?

    a. $10.40
    b. $8.60
    c. $14.90
    d. $23.40

12. The price of a book went up from $20 to $25. What percent did the price increase?

    a. 5%
    b. 10%
    c. 20%
    d. 25%

13. The price of a book decreased from $25 to $20. What percent did the price decrease?

    a. 5%
    b. 10%
    c. 20%
    d. 25%

14. A motorcycle travels at 50 km/hour for 25 minutes. How far does it travel?

    a. 10 km
    b. 20.83 km
    c. 25 km
    d. 22.85 km

15. A woman spends 3/5 of her salary on rent, and 1/6 on utilities and saves the rest. How much will she save in 1 year?

   a. 2 2/5 monthly salary
   b. 2 months salary
   c. 2 1/5 monthly salary
   c. 1 4/5 monthly salary

PART II - WRITTEN COMMUNICATIONS TEST WTI

Instructions: Read the following passage and write a concise summary in chronological order.

Scenario: Questioning a Suspect

Mr. Tom, a customer of Miss Polly's store was supposed to pick up his order on the 24th. Miss Polly's store was painted a bright yellow with beautiful posters on the wall. The suspect was a notorious tall 23 year old black man known as a local gang member. Miss Polly's store was between a flower shop and a coffee shop that offered 25% discounts on weekends. The suspect denied committing the crime but he didn't have any confirmable alibi. Miss Polly reported on the 23rd that her store has been broken into at night and some goods stolen. Witnesses reported that a tall young black man in a leather jacket and hood was seen lurking around the place after dark. The suspect's sister was a young beautiful lady who was married to the local baker. The suspect agreed to having committed the crime after shown the evidence against him. The security camera caught the image of someone as tall and black as the suspect committing the offence but his face was covered. The police picked up the suspect for questioning on the 25th. Miss Polly's store was located on Townsand Avenue. The description given by the witnesses fit the description of the suspect. Miss Poly took her kids to school and went to her store only to discover it broken into. A silver bracelet identified by Miss Polly as one of her stolen products was found on him. The suspect was wearing blue jeans, a black T-Shirt and white Nike sneakers when he was picked up. The hood used for the crime as seen on the security camera was found in the suspect's apartment.

PRACTICE TEST QUESTIONS 1   **129**

Answer Key

Police Analytical Thinking Inventory PATI

Part I - Deductive Reasoning
Section I - Syllogisms

1. A
True

2. B
False - Although all students carry a backpack, not everyone who carries a backpack is a student. i.e. there are some people who carry a backpack who are not students.

3. B
False – Just because all dogs are mammals does not mean that all mammals are dogs.

4. B
False – Based on the first 2 statements you could say that all felines are mammals, but you cannot say that all mammals are felines.

5. B
False

6. B
False

7. B
False – you cannot reach a negative conclusion from 2 positive statements

8. C
The only certain thing is Krizzia and Nea are related to each other.

9. A
The only certain thing is the villagers rely on fishing to earn money since they live near the ocean.

10. C
The only certain thing is Ben and Ted are inseparable.

11. B
The only certain thing is Karen is fond of gardening.

12. C
The only certain thing is Tom is a stamp collector.

13. D
The only certain thing is mother bought fruits and vegetables.

14. C
The only certain thing is they are twins.

15. A
The only certain thing is roses are fragrant.

SECTION II - MAPPING

1. D
The fastest route is through blocks X – A11 – A12 – A8 – A6. Time by car is 12 plus 2 minutes to buy gas is 14 minutes.

2. B
The fastest route is B – I – J – K – U – V. Time on foot is 42 minutes.

3. A
The Fastest route is A9 – A11 – A13 – A20. By bike the first two blocks would take 12 minutes. To walk the last block would take 6 minutes. Total time is 18 minutes.

4. D
Fastest route is Y – Z – A2 – A1 – A3 – A5 – A6 – A7. By car it would take 22 minutes.

5. B
Fastest route is H – S – Y – Z – A2 – A4. Time by bike is 26 minutes.

PRACTICE TEST QUESTIONS 1

6. B
The fastest route from Z to V is Z – A2- A4 – A6 – A8 – A7 – V. Total drive time is 16 minutes. From Z would go through 5 intersections. 15 seconds at each intersection is 45 seconds. Total time is 16 minutes, 45 seconds.

7. A
Driving from block Z to A12 would take 12 minutes.
Walking from block A to D would take 28 minutes
Driving from A to C and then walking to D would take 16 minutes
Riding a bike from block T to A14 would take 19 minutes.
The shortest trip would be driving from block Z to A12.

8. A
Walking from A3 to K would take 20 minutes
Riding a bike from A3 to A10 would take 11 minutes
Driving a car from A3 to S would take 11 minutes
Riding a bike from A3 to y, then driving a car to H would take 17 minutes
The most time would be to walk from A3 to K (A)

9. C
The shortest route from F to V is F – Q – W – V. The time on bike is 14 minutes.

10. A
Possible routes between F and V that goes through just 4 blocks are?
F – Q – R – X – W – V
F – E – O – P - W – V
F - E - O - Q - W – V
F - Q - W - P -N – V
F - Q - O - P - W – V
There are 5 possible routes.

11. C
There are 5 possible routes from block F to V that goes through just 4 blocks. 4 of the 5 routes take the least time of 17 minutes each.

12. B
The fastest route from H to X is H – K – N – V – W – X. On a bike that would take 27 minutes.

13. D
The fastest route from H to X is H – K – N – V – W – X. On foot for the first 3 blocks, it would take 9 minutes plus 11 minutes by bike to X. Total time is 20 minutes.

14. A
The fastest route is D – N – V – A7 – A8 - A6. To drive the first block is 3 minutes, then by bike the next 2 blocks is 11 minutes, and the on foot the last 2 blocks is 16 minutes. Total time is 30 minutes.

15. C
The fastest route is G – I – L – N – P. By bike it would take 20 minutes. Going through intersections I, L and N, is 3 minutes. Total time is 23 minutes.

PART II - INDUCTIVE REASONING

SECTION I - MATCHING

1. D
All the choice are buildings, (Church, School, Hospital) except police.

2. B
All the choice are for applying paint (paint brush, spray can, roller) except choice B, which is a fountain pen.

3. A
All the figures have four sides except choice A.

4. D
All the animals are mammals (human, whale, human) except choice D (fish).

5. B
All the numbers (25, 85, 40) are divisible by 5, except choice B, 68.

6. C
All the figures have straight lines in the top section except choice C which has diagonal lines.

7. C
All the figures have 2 rectangles in the top portion. One rectangle is divided in half, with half shaded, except choice C which has both halves shaded.

8. B
Each figure has a horizontal line in the upper segment except choice B, which has a vertical line.

9. A
All the signs are traffic directional signs (No Parking, Do Not Enter, Curve) except choice A (mountain).

10. A
All the choices have a flange which points inward, except choice A, which points outward.

11. D
All the numbers are primes (31, 37, 41) except choice D (46).

12. C
All the boxes have 6 dots except choice C which has 5.

13. C
One-quarter of the area is shaded in all choices except choice C.

14. B
All the fractions are reduced to the lowest terms except choice B (2/10 = 1/5).

15. C
All the figures have horizontal lines that are shorter than the vertical line except choice C.

SECTION II - SEQUENCES

1. B
The number of sides increases by one.

2. B
The shape rotates clockwise.

3. A
The top and bottom rows cycle forward and the middle row cycles backward.

4. D
The sum of the top two numbers is divided by subtracting the bottom two numbers.

5. C
The black box goes to the bottom and the t symbol rotates.

6. B
These are back to back letters in ascending alphabetical order.

7. C
In the upper row, one letter is missing, and in the bottom row, two letters are missing.

8. D
The triangle rotates clockwise and the numbers increase by three.

9. C
The first shape should be inside the second shape.

10. D
The third box contains two shapes which are present in both of the first two boxes.

11. A
The shape rotates counter-clockwise.

12. A

The arrow inside the box is the inverse of the previous one.
13. B
The number of points increases with each figure.

14. B
The larger, exterior figure is the smaller interior figure.

15. D
The number of stars increases by one, and the number of circles decreases by one.

Part III - Quantitative Reasoning

Section I - Basic Math

1. B
1518 ÷ 27 = 56 r6
To confirm: 56 * 27 = 1512

2. D
1628 / 4 =   407

3. A
143 * 4 = 572

4. B
7050 – 305 = 6745

5. B
305 * 25 = 7625

6. D
5x + 3 = 7x -1
First collect like terms on each side.
3 + 1 = 7x - 5x
4 - 2x
x = 2

7. C
5x + 2(x + 7) = 14x – 7.

5x + 2x + 14 = 14x - 7
7x + 14 = 14x - 7
Collect like terms.

14 + 7 = 14x - 7x
21 = 7x
x = 3

8. C
12t -10 = 14t +2.
Collect like terms
12t - 14t = 2 - 10
-2t = -8
t = 4

9. C
A common denominator is needed, a number which both 5 and 10 will divide into. So, 6+7/10 = 13/10 = 1 3/10.

10. A
A common denominator is needed, a number which both 15 and 10 will divide into. So 14-9/30 = 5/30 = 1/6.

11. C
3.57 - 3.21 = 0.36

12. B
To convert percent to decimal, simply divide the decimal by 100 or move the decimal point 2 places to the left. Therefore, 19 ÷ 100 = 0.19

13. A
To convert to percent, simply multiply the decimal by 100 or move the decimal point 2 places to the right. Therefore, 1.21 x 100 = 121%

14. A
To convert to percent, simply multiply the decimal by 100 or move the decimal point 2 places to the right. Therefore, 4.358 x 100 = 435.8%

15. D
9.065 - 4.071 = 4.994

Practice Test Questions 1   137

Section II - Problem Solving

1. B
Spent 15% - 100% - 15% = 85%

2. C
125 : 500 is the same as 25 : 100 or 1 : 4. So the amount of salt will be 0.75/4 = 0.1875, or about .19 grams.

3. B
Total expenses = 5284.34 + $8,384.76 + $2,920.00 = $16,589.10

Profit = revenue less expenses

$19,304.56 - 16589.10 = $2,715.46

4. A
$5,000 at 4% = 5000 X 4/100
5000 X .4 = 200
So the total after one year will be $5,200

5. C
If each bus carries 36 students, and there are 144 students total, then 144/36 = 4 buses.

6. D
If a square is 5 feet tall, then the area will be 5 X 5 = 25.

7. B
John's total will be 40% of 8.50 plus the tip of $1.30.

8.5 X 4/100 = 8.5 X .4 = 3.40

Total = 3.40 + 1.30 = $4.70.

8. D
If she has $8.75, that will equal 35 quarters. ($8.00 = 32 quarters and $.75 = 3 quarters, total 35 quarters).

She had 2 more quarters than she thought, so she had 35 - 2 = 33 quarters.

9. B

Suppose oranges in the basket before = x, Then: X + 8x/5 = 130, 5x + 8x = 650, so X = 50.

10. D

As price of all the single items is same and there are 13 total items. So the total cost will be 13 × 1.3 = $16.90. After 3.5 percent tax this amount will become 16.9×1.035=$17.50.

11. B

The distribution is at three different rates and amounts:

$6.4 per 20 kilograms to 15 shops ... 20•15 = 300 kilograms distributed

$3.4 per 10 kilograms to 12 shops ... 10•12 = 120 kilograms distributed

550 - (300 + 120) = 550 - 420 = 130 kilograms left. This amount is distributed by 5 kilogram portions. So, this means that there are 130/5 = 26 shops.

$1.8 per 130 kilograms.

We need to find the amount he earned overall these distributions.

$6.4 per 20 kilograms : 6.4 * 15 = $96 for 300 kilograms

$3.4 per 10 kilograms : 3.4 * 12 = $40.8 for 120 kilograms

$1.8 per 5 kilograms : 1.8 * 26 = $46.8 for 130 kilograms

So, he earned 96 + 40.8 + 46.8 = $ 183.6

The total cost of distribution is given as $10

The profit is found by: Money earned - money spent ... It is important to remember that he bought 550 kilograms of potatoes for $165 at the beginning:

Profit = 183.6 - 10 - 165 = $8.60

12. D

The price increased by $5 ($25-$20). The percent increase is 5/20 x 100 = 5 x 5=25%

13. C

The price decreased by $5 ($25-$20). The percent increase = 5/25 x 100 = 5 x 4 =20%.

14. B

50 km/hour is 50/60 per minute = 0.8333 km/hour, so in 25 minutes it will travel 25 * 0.8333 = 20.83 km.

15. A

Setup the equation - 3/5 + 1/6 + X = 1
Find a common denominator 18/30 + 5/30 + X = 1
23/30 + X = 1
X = 1 - 23/30
X = 7/30 (amount of monthly savings)
so in 1 year she will save 12 X 7/30 = 84/30
= 2 12/30 = 2 2/5

PART II - WRITTEN COMMUNICATIONS TEST WTI

Suggested Summary

The Break In

Miss Polly reported on the 23rd that her store has been broken into at night and some goods stolen.

The police picked up the suspect for questioning on the 25th.

Evidence

Witnesses reported that a tall young black man in a leather jacket and hood was seen lurking around the place after dark.

The security camera caught the image of someone as tall and black as the suspect committing the offence but his face was covered.

The hood used for the crime as seen on the security camera was found in the suspect's apartment.

The description given by the witnesses fit the description of the suspect.

A silver bracelet identified by Miss Polly as one of her stolen products was found on him.

Questioning the Suspect

The suspect denied committing the crime but he didn't have any confirmable alibi.

The suspect agreed to having committed the crime after shown the evidence against him.

Details (Not included in report)

Miss Polly's store was located on Townsend Avenue.
Mr. Tom, a customer of Miss Polly's store was supposed to pick up his order on the 24th.

Miss Polly's store was painted a bright yellow with beautiful posters on the wall.

Miss Polly's store was between a flower shop and a coffee shop that offered 25% discounts on weekends.

The suspect's sister was a young beautiful lady who was married to the local baker.

Miss Poly took her kids to school and went to her store only to discover it broken into.

The suspect was wearing blue jeans, a black t-shirt and white Nike sneakers when he was picked up.

PRACTICE TEST QUESTIONS SET 2

The questions below are not the same as you will find on the Ontario Police Exam - that would be too easy! And nobody knows what the questions will be and they change all the time. Below are general questions that cover the same subject areas as the exam. So, while the format and exact wording of the questions may differ slightly, and change from year to year, if you can answer the questions below, you will have no problem with the exam.

For the best results, take these Practice Test Questions as if it were the real exam. Set aside time when you will not be disturbed, and a location that is quiet and free of distractions. Read the instructions carefully, read each question carefully, and answer to the best of your ability.
Use the bubble answer sheets provided. When you have completed the Practice Questions, check your answer against the Answer Key and read the explanation provided.

Do not attempt more than one set of practice test questions in one day. After completing the first practice test, wait two or three days before attempting the second set of questions.

PRACTICE TEST QUESTIONS 2   **143**

POLICE ANALYTICAL THINKING INVENTORY PATI

Part I - Deductive Reasoning

    Syllogisms - 15 Questions

    Mapping - 15 Questions

Part II - Inductive Reasoning

    Matching - 15 questions

    Sequences - 15 questions

Part III Quantitative Reasoning

    Basic Math - 15 questions

    Problem Solving - 15 Questions

WRITTEN COMMUNICATION TEST WCT

1 question

Syllogism Answer Sheet

	A	B	C	D
1	○	○	○	○
2	○	○	○	○
3	○	○	○	○
4	○	○	○	○
5	○	○	○	○
6	○	○	○	○
7	○	○	○	○
8	○	○	○	○
9	○	○	○	○
10	○	○	○	○
11	○	○	○	○
12	○	○	○	○
13	○	○	○	○
14	○	○	○	○
15	○	○	○	○

Mapping Answer Sheet

	A	B	C	D
1	○	○	○	○
2	○	○	○	○
3	○	○	○	○
4	○	○	○	○
5	○	○	○	○
6	○	○	○	○
7	○	○	○	○
8	○	○	○	○
9	○	○	○	○
10	○	○	○	○
11	○	○	○	○
12	○	○	○	○
13	○	○	○	○
14	○	○	○	○
15	○	○	○	○

Matching Answer Sheet

	A	B	C	D
1	○	○	○	○
2	○	○	○	○
3	○	○	○	○
4	○	○	○	○
5	○	○	○	○
6	○	○	○	○
7	○	○	○	○
8	○	○	○	○
9	○	○	○	○
10	○	○	○	○
11	○	○	○	○
12	○	○	○	○
13	○	○	○	○
14	○	○	○	○
15	○	○	○	○

Sequences Answer Sheet

	A	B	C	D
1	○	○	○	○
2	○	○	○	○
3	○	○	○	○
4	○	○	○	○
5	○	○	○	○
6	○	○	○	○
7	○	○	○	○
8	○	○	○	○
9	○	○	○	○
10	○	○	○	○
11	○	○	○	○
12	○	○	○	○
13	○	○	○	○
14	○	○	○	○
15	○	○	○	○

Basic Math Answer Sheet

	A	B	C	D
1	○	○	○	○
2	○	○	○	○
3	○	○	○	○
4	○	○	○	○
5	○	○	○	○
6	○	○	○	○
7	○	○	○	○
8	○	○	○	○
9	○	○	○	○
10	○	○	○	○
11	○	○	○	○
12	○	○	○	○
13	○	○	○	○
14	○	○	○	○
15	○	○	○	○

Problem Solving Answer Sheet

	A	B	C	D
1	○	○	○	○
2	○	○	○	○
3	○	○	○	○
4	○	○	○	○
5	○	○	○	○
6	○	○	○	○
7	○	○	○	○
8	○	○	○	○
9	○	○	○	○
10	○	○	○	○
11	○	○	○	○
12	○	○	○	○
13	○	○	○	○
14	○	○	○	○
15	○	○	○	○

Police Analytical Thinking Inventory
PATI

Part I - Deductive Reasoning
Section I - Syllogisms

1.
All colonels are officers.
All officers are soldiers.
No colonels are soldiers.

If the first 2 statements are true, then the third statement is:

   a. True
   b. False
   c. Uncertain

2.
No houses on Appleby Street or Francisco streets cost more than $500,000. My house is not on Appleby or Francisco Street.

My house does not cost more than $500,000.

If the first 2 statements are true, then the third statement is:

   a. True
   b. False
   c. Uncertain

3.
Some tropical fish are very sensitive.
I have many types of tropical fish. Some of my fish are very sensitive.

If the first 2 statements are true, then the third statement is:

   a. True
   b. False
   c. Uncertain

4.
Most people in oil producing countries are rich.

I live in an oil producing country.
I am rich.

If the first 2 statements are true, then the third statement is:

   a. True
   b. False
   c. Uncertain

5.
Science can explain all events. Making a decision is an event. Science cannot explain how I make a decision.

If the first 2 statements are true, then the third statement is:

   a. True
   b. False
   c. Uncertain

6.
Doctors can sometimes predict epidemics.

Bird Flu is becoming an epidemic. Doctors know where bird flu will spread.

If the first 2 statements are true, then the third statement is:

    a. True

    b. False

    c. Uncertain

7.
That store sells new and used books.
My textbook is used.
My textbook came from that store.

If the first 2 statements are true, then the third statement is:

    a. True

    b. False

    c. Uncertain

8. Angel gets the highest grades in all the subjects in school. She is also the president of the student body. Every year she gets the highest award given by the school.

    a. Angel is a slow learner.

    b. Everybody admires Angel.

    c. Other children are envious of Angel.

    d. Angel is at the top of her class.

9. John is fond of the color green. He always wears green shirts to school. His rubber shoes are also green. His bag, raincoat, and notebooks are also green

    a. John has green eyes.

    b. John hates the color green.

    c. John like the color green.

    d. John wears blue rubber shoes to school.

10. The Earth is the only planet with known life forms. It is the third planet from the sun in the solar system. It rotates on its axis in 24 hours and revolves around the sun in 365 ¼ days.

    a. There is no life on Earth.

    b. The Earth is round.

    c. The Earth is the farthest planet in the solar system.

    d. Many living things live on Earth.

11. Rhea helps mother with the household chores everyday. She sweeps the floor every morning. She also helps mother prepare food for the family. She washes the dishes too.

    a. Rhea is helpful.

    b. Rhea is too lazy to do household chores.

    c. Rhea waters the plants.

    d. Rhea cooks for the whole family.

12. The children enjoy playing football after school. Sometimes, they play basketball with other kids. On weekends, they play baseball, badminton, or tennis.

    a. Children prefer playing indoors.

    b. Children enjoy different kinds of sports.

    c. Children hate playing.

    d. Playing is a form of exercise.

13. Jane spends her free time reading. She likes to read books, magazines, and even newspapers. She reads stories about adventures and fairy tales.

    a. Jane likes to watch television.

    b. Jane spends her free time writing stories.

    c. Jane's hobby is reading.

    d. Jane reads stories in school.

14. The body is made up of many bones. The skull protects the head. The ribs protect the chest. There are also small bones that protect the ears.

    a. Bones are connected to the muscles.

    b. Bones are present in the stomach.

    c. Animals have bones.

    d. Bones protect different parts of the body.

15. Trees give off oxygen. They also provide shade during sunny days. Some trees bear fruits while others are used to build houses.

    a. Trees have many purposes.
    b. Trees aren't important to men.
    c. Birds build nests in trees.
    d. Roots and trunk are parts of a tree.

Section II - Mapping

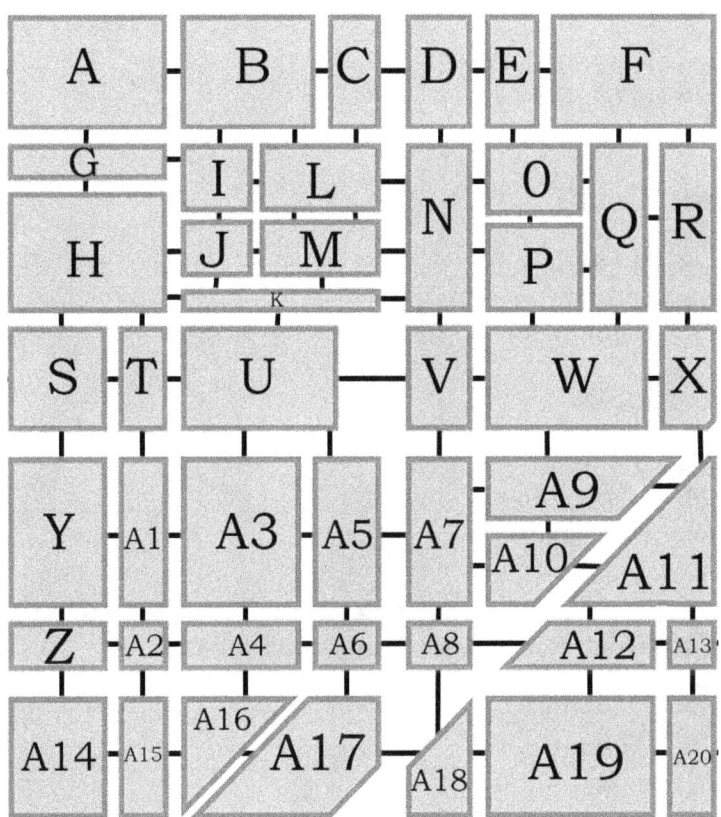

Map Key

Each Square labeled A to Z and A1 to A20 represent the corner of an intersection. The lines between the squares represent a city block. The intersections and city blocks fall into 3 categories.

Large blocks: A, B,F, H, N, Q, R, U, W, Y, A3, A5, A7, A9, A11, A14, A17, A19

Small blocks: C, D, E, I. J, L,M, O, P, S, T, V, X, A1, A4, A10, Z, A12, A15, A16, A18, A20

Mini blocks: G, K, A2, A6, A8, A13

The time it takes to travel from one city block to another is:

Large blocks

In a car: 4 minutes
On a bike: 6 minutes
On foot: 10 minutes

Small Blocks

In a car: 3 minutes
On a bike: 5 minutes
On foot: 8 minutes

Mini Blocks

In a car: 2 minutes
On a bike: 4 minutes
On foot: 6 minutes

1. A girl rides a bike from A12 to A5 and returns to A12 by a different route. How long would it take?

    a. 35 minutes

    b. 37 minutes

    c. 39 minutes

    d. 28 minutes

2. There is a parade and block O is closed to vehicles. A driver starts at block N and drives to R. Then he has to return to N by a different route. How fast could he accomplish this?

    a. 20 minutes

    b. 11 minutes

    c. 27 minutes

    d. 25 minutes

3. A man rides a bike from A18 to block N and then returns via the same route. How long would it take him if he used the fastest route?

   a. 41 minutes
   b. 38 minutes
   c. 44 minutes
   d. 29 minutes

4. A police patrol team drove from A3 to A10, with a 30 seconds stop at each intersection in between. From A10 it then drove to block W without spending any extra time at the intersections. How long would the trip take using the fastest route?

   a. 19 minutes, 30 seconds
   b. 18 minutes
   c. 20 minutes
   d. 21 minutes, 45 seconds

5. A delivery van goes from block U to A4. How fast would it take, it if it had to go through block V and spend an extra 15 seconds each time it has to make a turn at an intersection?

   a. 15 minutes, 30 seconds
   b. 15 minutes, 15 seconds
   c. 17 minutes, 30 seconds
   d. 16 minutes, 30 seconds

6. A group of 4 students move from block F to block A. How fast can they go if they drive a car the first 2 blocks, ride their bikes the next 2 blocks and walk the rest of the way?

   a. 25 minutes
   b. 27 minutes
   c. 30 minutes
   d. 29 minutes

7. A car drives from block R to A10. Using the fastest route, how long would it take if it spends 30 seconds each time it has to turn at an intersection?

   a. 6 minutes
   b. 7 minutes
   c. 10 minutes, 30 seconds
   d. 7 minutes, 30 seconds

8. Using the fastest route, a bike ride from V to A18 and then a car ride to A4 through A16 would take how long?

   a. 25 minutes
   b. 22 minutes
   c. 28 minutes
   d. 24 minutes

9. A boy rides his bike from S to K but gets lost along the way. What is the shortest time it would have taken him if his trip took him through blocks J and L?

   a. 20 minutes
   b. 22 minutes
   c. 23 minutes
   d. 25 minutes

10. Which of the following would be the shortest trip?

    a. Bike ride from D to V
    b. Walking from O to W
    c. Driving a car from B to A3
    d. They all take the same time

11. A bike race starts from block U and finishes at block A18. If the race has to pass through blocks V and A6, what is the shortest possible time to complete the race?

   a. 29 minutes
   b. 34 minutes
   c. 30 minutes
   d. 31 minutes

12. There is traffic congestion around blocks N, V, A7 and A8. Cars can't get through, and drivers need to park and walk. A car driver heads for block A12 from U. How quickly can they get there?

   a. 19 minutes
   b. 17 minutes
   c. 21 minutes
   d. 18 minutes

13. How long will it take to walk from block T to block A15 if you must walk through A16?

   a. 38 minutes
   b. 41 minutes
   c. 42 minutes
   d. 37 minutes

14. How long will it take to drive a car from S to W?

   a. 6 minutes
   b. 12 minutes
   c. 18 minutes
   d. 13 minutes

15. How long to ride a bike from block G to block O?

a. 24 minutes
b. 19 minutes
c. 20 minutes
d. 21 minutes

PART II - INDUCTIVE REASONING

SECTION I - MATCHING

Directions: In each of the following questions, select the choice that does not belong with the other three.

1.

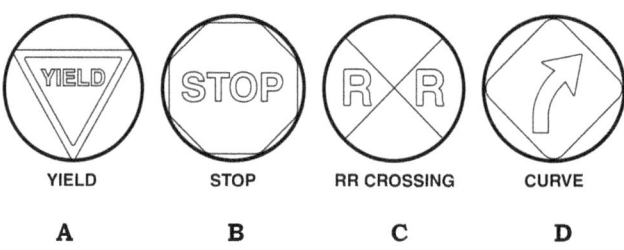

YIELD	STOP	RR CROSSING	CURVE
A	B	C	D

2.

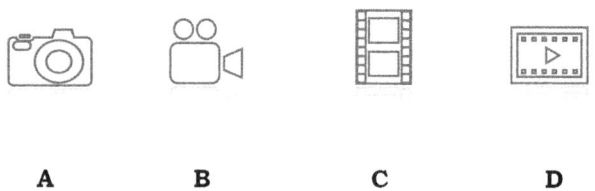

| A | B | C | D |

3.

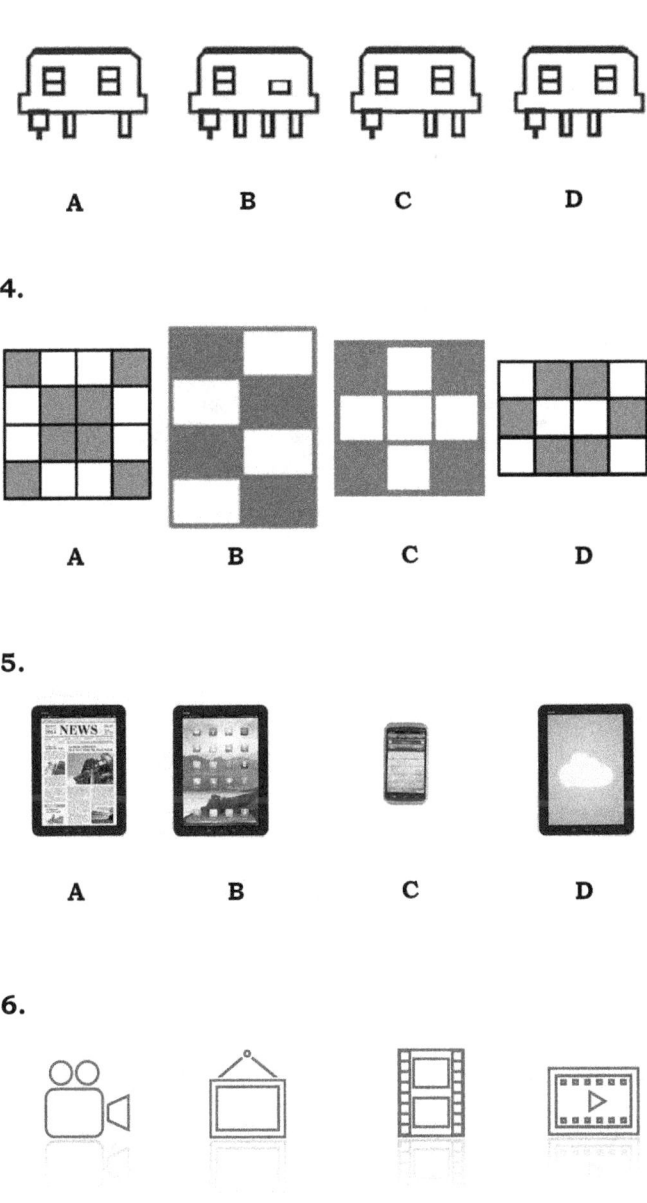

4.

5.

6.

7.

AD　HK　QS　WZ

　　A　　　B　　　C　　　D

8.

17　68　84　34

　　A　　　B　　　C　　　D

9.

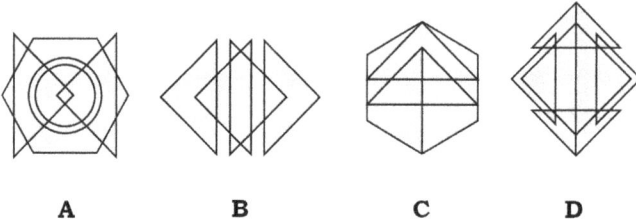

　　A　　　B　　　C　　　D

10.

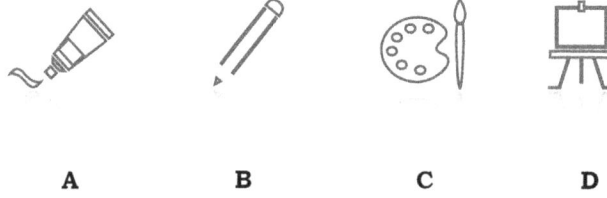

　　A　　　B　　　C　　　D

11.

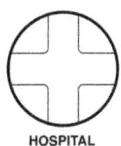   

    A   B   C   D

12.

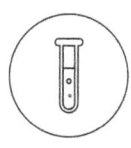   

    A   B   C   D

13.

 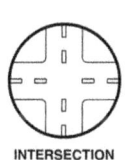  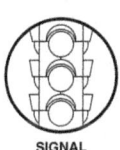

STOP   INTERSECTION   CONSTRUCTION   SIGNAL

    A   B   C   D

14.

    A   B   C   D

164

15.

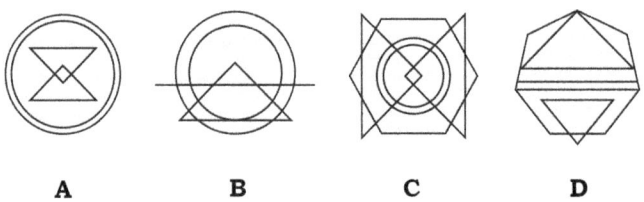

A   B   C   D

SECTION II - SEQUENCES

1.

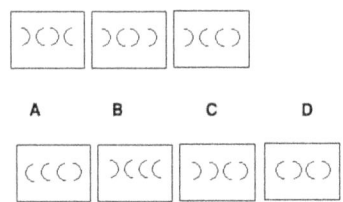

2.

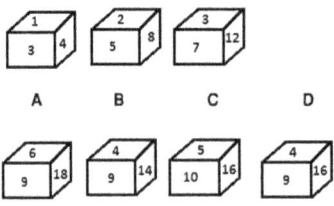

3.

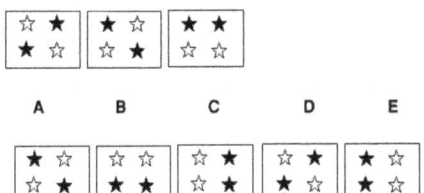

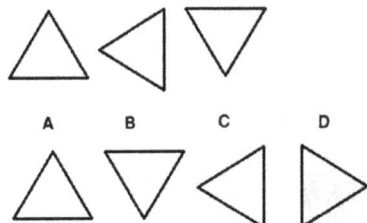

4.

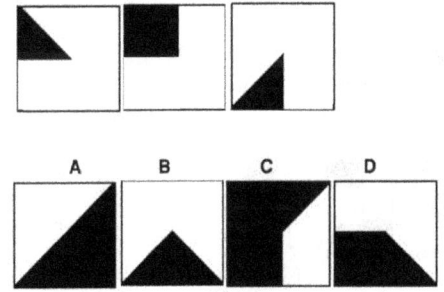

5.

6.

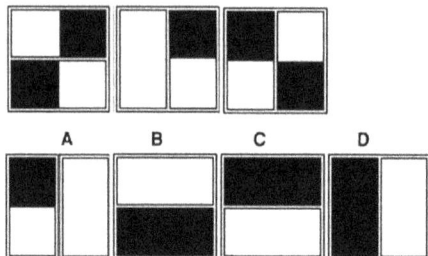

7.

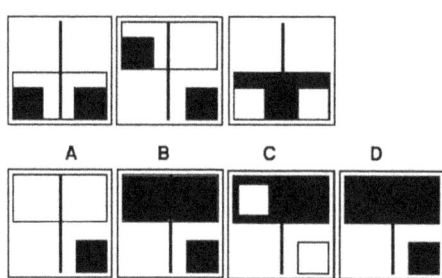

8.

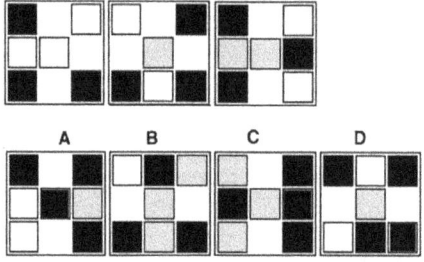

9.

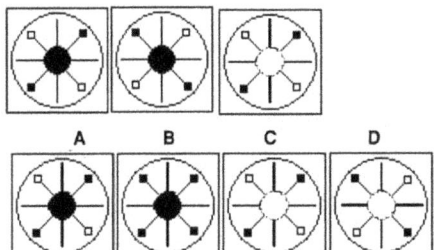

10.

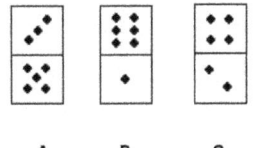

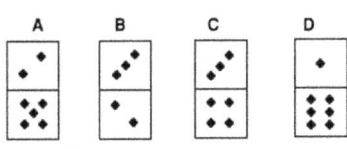

11.

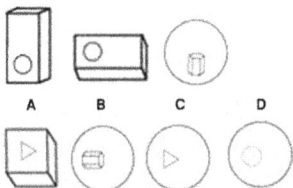

12.

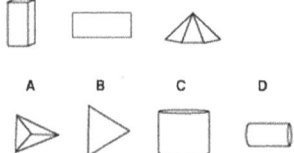

13.

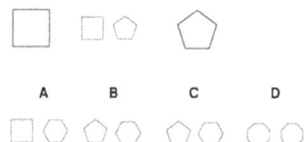

14.

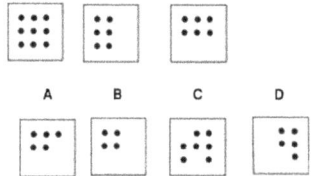

15.

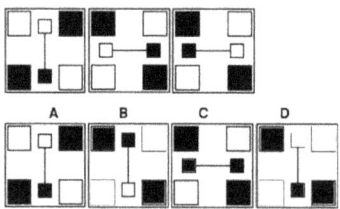

Part III - Quantitative Reasoning

Section I - Basic Math

1. 1210 / 5

    a. 342
    b. 232
    c. 242
    d. 240

2. 8327 − 1278 =

    a. 7149
    b. 7209
    c. 6059
    d. 7049

3. 294 / 21 =

    a. 21
    b. 14
    c. 28
    d. 56

4. 1278 + 4920 =

    a. 6298
    b. 6108
    c. 6198
    d. 6098

5. 5/9 + 2/9

    a. 6/11
    b. 1 3/7
    c. 7/18
    d. 7/9

6. 6/10 x 5/16

    a. 4/15
    b. 3/16
    c. 2 1/3
    d. 2/7

7. 2/15 ÷ 4/5

    a. 6/65
    b. 6/75
    c. 5/12
    d. 1/6

8. Express 71/1000 as a decimal.

    a. .71
    b. .0071
    c. .071
    d. 7.1

9. 4.7 + .9 + .01 =

    a. 5.5
    b. 6.51
    c. 5.61
    d. 5.7

10. .33 × .59 =

    a. .1947

    b. 1.947

    c. .0197

    d. .1817

11. Solve for x. 5x + 21 = 66.

    a. 19

    b. 9

    c. 15

    d. 5

12. If X + (32 + 356) = 920. What is x?

    a. 450

    b. 388

    c. 532

    d. 623

13. Solve for x. (12 x 12)/x = 12

    a. 12

    b. 13

    c. 8

    d. 14

14. Solve for A. A − (34 x 2) = 18.

    a. 86

    b. 78

    c. 50

    d. 73

15. Solve for X. X% of 120 = 30.

   a. 15
   b. 12
   c. 4
   d. 25

Section II - Problem Solving

1. Richard sold 12 shirts for total revenue of $336 at 8% profit. What is the purchase price of each shirt?

   a. $25.76
   b. $24.50
   c. $23.75
   d. $22.50

2. In a local election at polling station A, 945 voters cast their vote out of 1270 registered voters. At polling station B, 860 cast their vote out of 1050 registered voters and at station C, 1210 cast their vote out of 1440 registered voters. What was the total turnout including all three polling stations?

   a. 70%
   b. 74%
   c. 76%
   d. 80%

3. In a factory, the average salary of all employees is $125. The average salary of 10 managers is $300 and average salary of workers is $100. What is the total number of employees?

   a. 30
   b. 40
   c. 25
   d. 50

4. In a 30 minute test there are 40 problems. A student solved 28 problems in first 25 minutes. How many seconds should she give to each of the remaining problems?

    a. 20 seconds
    b. 23 seconds
    c. 25 seconds
    d. 27 seconds

5. The total cost of building a fence around a square field is $2000 at a rate of $5 per meter. What is the length of one side?

    a. 80 meters
    b. 100 meters
    c. 40 meters
    d. 320 meters

6. In a class of 83 students, 72 are present. What percent of student is absent? Provide answer up to two significant digits.

    a. 12
    b. 13
    c. 14
    d. 15

7. The price of a product was increased by 45%. If the initial cost of the product was $220, what is the new cost of the product?

    a. $230
    b. $300
    c. $319
    d. $245

8. A worker's weekly salary was increased by 30%. If his new salary is $150, what was his old salary?

   a. $120.00
   b. $99.15
   c. $109.00
   d. $115.40

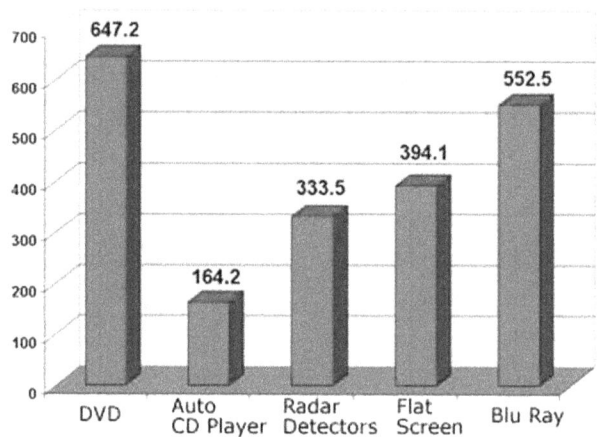

9. Consider the graph above. What is the third best-selling product?

   a. Radar Detectors
   b. Flat Screen TV
   c. Blu Ray
   d. Auto CD Players

10. Which two products are the closest in the number of sales?

   a. Blu Ray and Flat Screen TV
   b. Flat Screen TV and Radar Detectors
   c. Radar Detectors and Auto CD Players
   d. DVD players and Blu Ray

11. Great Britain has a Value Added Tax of 15%. A shop sells a camera for $545. If the VAT is included in the price, what is the actual cost of the camera?

    a. $490.40

    b. $473.90

    c. $505.00

    d. $503.15

12. The owner of a pet store decided to increase the cost of all reptiles 45%. If the initial cost of a reptile was $220, what is the new cost?

    a. $230

    b. $300

    c. $319

    d. $245

13. 5 men have to share a load weighing 10kg 550g equally among themselves. How much will each man have to carry?

    a. 900 g

    b. 1.5 kg

    c. 3 kg

    d. 2 kg 110 g

14. Peter drives 4 blocks to school and back every day. How many blocks does he drive in 5 days?

    a. 20

    b. 30

    c. 40

    d. 50

15. How much pay does Mr. Johnson receive if he gives half to his family, pays $250 for rent, and has exactly 3/7 of his pay left over?

    a. $3,600
    b. $2,800
    c. $1,750
    d. $3,500

Part II - Written Communications Test WTI

Instructions: Read the following passage and write a concise summary in chronological order.

Scenario: Responding to a Call

She was watching her favorite TV show and got up during commercials to use the toilet when she noticed the car from the toilet window. Mrs. Polly called the police around 7 am to report some suspicious activity in her neighborhood. Lights were on inside the house and she was sure that some other people were inside the house. Her home was a tidy small apartment with several family picture photos on her wall. She told her daughter about it in the morning and she advised her to report the matter to the police. They went inside her house where she offered the detective tea and biscuits. A police team arrived at Mrs. Polly's house on Storybrooke rd. by 7.45 to question her. The opposite house was a three bedroom apartment and was painted while and yellow. Mrs. Polly had noticed a white Mercedes parked at the house opposite at around 10.15 pm the night before. The police team found Mrs. Polly at her garden by her house tending to her flowers. Two men in dark coats and hats were waiting by the car and they kept looking up and down the street. Mrs. Polly is a grandmother and her daughter has gone to the local school where she teaches. She found it strange because she knew that the couple at that house who were her friends had gone on holidays to see their son in Canada. She was wearing a bright yellow dress when detectives Marci Gonzalez and Paul White arrived. The police saw a photo of her late husband in his military uniform. The detectives asked questions about what she wanted to report. The detective confirmed that she had a clear view of the opposite house from the toilet window. Her granddaughter of about 2 years was asleep inside. She called the house several times while the men were there, but no one picked the phone. Detective Garcia Gonzalez had a son who was a student at the school where Mrs. Polly's daughter teachers.

Answer Key

1. False
Both premises to this argument use 'all,' so the conclusion (which uses 'no') must be false.

2. Uncertain
No information is given about houses NOT on Appleby or Francisco streets.

3. Uncertain
It is possible that some of my tropical fish are very sensitive, but it is also possible that they are all insensitive varieties.

4. Uncertain
I may be rich or I may not be.

5. False
IF Science can explain all events, AND making a decision is an event, THEN science CAN explain how I make a decision.

6. False.
There are 2 problems. Doctors can sometimes predict epidemics. Bird Flu is becoming an epidemic.

Bird flu is not an epidemic yet, and doctors can only predict epidemics sometimes.

7. Uncertain.
My textbook MAY have come from that store or it may have come from another store.

8. D
The only certain thing is Angel is at the top of her class.

9. C
The only certain thing is John likes color green.

10. D
The only certain thing is many living things live on Earth.

11. A
The only certain thing is Rhea is helpful.

12. C
The only certain thing is children enjoy different kinds of sports.

13. C
The only certain thing is Jane's hobby is reading.

14. D
The only certain thing is bones protect different parts of the body.

15. A
The only certain thing is trees have many purposes.

SECTION II - MAPPING

1. B
The fastest route is A12 – A8 – A6 – A5 which takes 14 minutes. To return, A5 – A7 – A10 – A11 – A12 takes 23 minutes. Total time is 37 minutes.

2. D
The route to R is, N – P – Q – R which takes 11 minutes. The route back, avoiding O, is R – X – W – V which takes 14 minutes. Total time is 25 minutes.

3. A
The fastest route is A18 – A8 – A7 – V – N – V – A7 – A8 – A18. Total time is 41 minutes.

4. C
The fastest route is A3 – A5 – A7 – A10, which takes 12 minutes. 30 seconds stop at A5 and A7 is one minute. From A10 - A9 – W takes 7 minutes. Total time is 20 minutes.

5. A
The fastest route from U to A4 through V, is U – V – A7 – A8 – A6 – A4 and it takes 15 minutes. The car makes a turn at V and A8, that is 30 seconds. Total is 15 minutes, 30 seconds.

6. B
The fastest route is F – E – D – C – B – A. The first 2 blocks by car will take 7 minutes. The next 2 blocks by bike will take 10 minutes, the last block on foot would take 10 minutes. Total time 27 minutes.

7. D
The fastest route is R – X – A11 – A10 and it takes 7 minutes by car. He makes a turn at A11 for 30 seconds. Total time is 7 minutes, 30 seconds.

8. A
The fastest route is V – A7 – A8 – A18. By bike would take 15 minutes. From A18 through A16 to A14 by car would go through A18 – A17 – A16 – A4. By car would take 10 minutes. Total time is 25 minutes.

9. C
The shortest route is S – H – J – I – L – M – K. By bike it would take 23 minutes.

10. D
From D to V by bike would take 16 minutes. Walking from O to W would take 16 minutes. From B to A3 by car would take 16 minutes. So all three routes would take same time.

11. D
The fastest route that goes through V and A6 is U – V – A7 – A8 – A6 – A17 – A18. By bike would take 31 minutes.

12. B
The fastest route is U – A5 – A6 – A8. By car it would take 11 minutes. Then on foot to A12 would take 6 minutes. Total time is 17 minutes.

13. A
Fastest route is T – A1 – A2 – A4 – A16 – A15. Time on foot is 38 minutes.

14. D
Best route is S – T – U – V – W in 13 minutes.

15. C
The fastest route is G – I – L – N – O, which would take 20 minutes by bike.

Part II - Inductive Reasoning

Section I - Matching

1. C
All signs are directional road signs except choice C

2. A
All figures are film or movie related except choice A.

3. B
Choice B has 3 prongs and a half rectangle in the upper portion.

4. C
All figures have half-shaded except choice C.

5. C
All figures are tablets except choice C which is a phone.

6. B
All figures are movie related except choice B.

7. C
All letter combinations are separated by 2 letters (e.g. A, B, C, D), except choice C QS.

8. C
All letters are multiples of 17 except choice C, 84.

9. A
Choice A is the only figure which a circle.

10. B
All figures are related to painting, except choice B (pencil).

11. D
Although the symbol is medical related, it is not hospital related.

12. D
All the symbols are laboratory related except choice D (crutches).

13. C
While choice C is a road sign, it is not related to an intersection like the other choices.

14. A
All the figures are medical assist except choice A.

15. D
All the choices have a circle except choice D.

SECTION II - SEQUENCES

1. C
The half circles rotate 180 degrees from right to left.

2. D
The numbers on top are increasing by one, the number on the front are increasing by 2 and the numbers on the right are multiple of 4.

3. B
Two black stars are placed in the opposite direction to the previous.

4. D
The triangle rotates counter-clockwise.

5. B
A triangle is added to the existing triangle to create a square in the second figure, and a larger triangle in choice B.

6. A
The bottom square is deleted each time.

7. C
The large rectangle and one squares move to the top.

8. B
One white square turns grey.

9. D
The figure rotates counter-clockwise.

10. B
The total number of dots decreases by 1 each time.

11. B
The figures is rotated clock-wise.

12. B
The figure is rotated clockwise and goes from 3-dimensional to 2-dimentional.

13. B
An additional figure with one more side is added. (E.g. 4 sides to 5 sides, 5 sides to 6 sides).

14. B
One-third of the dots are deleted.

15. A
The figure rotates counter-clockwise.

Part III - Quantitative Reasoning

Section I - Basic Math

1. C
1210 / 5 = 242

2. D
8327 − 1278 = 7049

3. B
294 / 21 = 14

4. C
1278 + 4920 = 6198

5. D
Since the denominators are the same, we can just add the numerators, so (5+2)/9 = 7/9.

6. B
Since there are common numerators and denominators to cancel out, we cancel out 6/10 x 5/16 to get 6/2 x 1/16 = 3/2 x 1/8, and then we multiply numerators and denominators to get 3/16

6. B
6/10 X 5/16. First cancel common terms in the numerator and denominator.

3/2 X 1/8 Multiply through.

(3 X 1) / (2 X 8) = 3/16.

7. D
To divide fractions, we multiply the first fraction with the inverse of the second fraction. Therefore we have 2/15 x 5/4, (cancel out) = 1/3 x ½ = 1/6

8. C
Converting a fraction to a decimal – divide the numerator by the denominator – so 71/1000 = .071. Dividing by 1000 moves the decimal point 3 places.

9. C
4.7 + .9 + .01 = 5.61

10. A
.33 × .59 = .1947

11. B
5x + 21 = 66, 5x = 66 − 21 = 45, 5x = 45, x = 45/5 = 9

12. C
32 + 356 = 388. Therefore X + 388 = 920, X = 920 − 388 = 532

13. A
12 x 12 = 144, so 144/x = 12
144 = 12X
X = 12

14. A
34 x 2 = 68, so A − 68 = 18, A = 68 + 18 = 86

15. D
X% of 120 = 30, so X = 30/120 x 100/1 = 300/12 = 25

Section II - Problem Solving

1. A
The price of 12 shirts with profit is 8% = 0.92 X 336 = $309.12 The purchase price of each shirt = 309.12/12 = $25.76

2. D
To find the total turnout in all three polling stations, we need to proportion the number of voters to the number of all registered voters.
Number of total voters = 945 + 860 + 1210 = 3015

Number of total registered voters = 1270 + 1050 + 1440 = 3760

Percentage turnout over all three polling stations = 3015 * 100/3760 = 80.19%

Checking the answers, we round 80.19 to the nearest whole number: 80%

3. B
Assume the total numbers of employees is x. The total salary of all employees will be 125x. The total salary of the managers = 10 X 300 = $3000. The number of employees =

X - 10, so the total salary of employees will be 100 X (X-10). The equation becomes 100(X - 10) + 3000 = 125X. x = 40.

4. C
The number of remaining questions is 40 - 28 = 12
The time remaining is 30 - 25 = 5 minutes = 5 X 60 = 300 seconds. So the time remaining for each question is 300/12 = 25 seconds.

5. B
Total expense is $2000 and we are informed that $5 is spent per meter. Combining these two information, we know that the total length of the fence is 2000/5 = 400 meters.

The fence is built around a square-shaped field. If one side of the square is "a," the perimeter of the square is "4a." Here, the perimeter is equal to 400 meters. So,

400 = 4a

100 = a → this means that one side of the square is equal to 100 meters.

6. B
If 72 students are present, then 83 - 72 = 11 students are absent. To calculate the percent, the equation will be,

11/83 = x/100
83x = 1100
x = 1100/83
x = 13.25   rounding off - 13% of the students are absent.

7. C
Initial cost was $220. New cost = 220 + (45% of 220), 45% of 220, 45/100 x 220 = 99, therefore new price is 220 + 99 = $319

8. D
Let old salary = X, therefore $150 = x + 0.30x, 150 = 1x + 0.30x, 150 = 1.30x, x = 150/1.30 = 115.4

9. B
Flat Screen TVs are the third best-selling product.

10. B
The two products that are closest in the number of sales, are Flat Screen TVs and Radar Detectors.

11. B
Actual cost = X, therefore, 545 = x + 0.15x, 545 = 1x + 0.15x, 545 = 1.15x, x = 545/1.15 = 473.9

12. C
Initial cost was $220. New cost = 200 + 45% of 200, 45% of 200, 45/100 x 220 = 99, therefore new price is 220 + 99 = $319

13. D
First convert the unit of measurements to be the same. Since 1000 g = 1 kg, 10 kg = 10 x 1000 = 10,000 + 550 g = 10,550 g. Divide 10,550 among 5 = 10550/5 = 2110 = 2 kg 110 g

14. C
Each round trip will be 8 blocks, so in 5 days, he will drive 5 X 8 = 40 blocks.

15. D
The equation will be, X/2 – 250 = 3X/7
X = $3,500.

Part II - Written Communications Test
WTI

Suggested Summary - Sort out the details that are not important to the report, and simplify and write out the important facts.

Chronology

Mrs. Polly had noticed a white Mercedes parked at the house opposite at around 10.15 pm the night before. Lights were on inside the house and she was sure that some other people were inside the house.

She found it strange because she knew that the couple at that house who were her friends had gone on holidays to see their son in Canada.

Mrs. Polly noticed the car and suspicious activity at 7 am.

Two men in dark coats and hats were waiting by the car and they kept looking up and down the street.

She called the house several times while the men were there but no one picked the phone.

A police team (Marci Gonzalez and Paul White) arrived at Mrs. Polly's house on Storybrooke Rd. at 7.45.

The detective confirmed that she had a clear view of the opposite house from the toilet window.

DETAILS

She was watching her favorite TV show and got up during commercials to use the toilet when she noticed the car from the toilet window.

Her home was a tidy small apartment with several family picture photos on her wall.

She told her daughter about it in the morning and she advised her to report the matter to the police.

They went inside her house where she offered the detective tea and biscuits.

The opposite house was a three bedroom apartment and was painted while and yellow. The police team found Mrs. Polly at her garden by her house tending to her flowers.

Mrs. Polly is a grandmother and her daughter has gone to the local school where she teaches.

The police saw a photo of her late husband in his military uniform. The detectives asked questions about what she wanted to report.

Her granddaughter of about 2 years was asleep inside. Detective Garcia Gonzalez had a son who was a student at the school where Mrs. Polly's daughter teachers.

Conclusion

CONGRATULATIONS! You have made it this far because you have applied yourself diligently to practicing for the exam and no doubt improved your potential score considerably! Getting into a good school is a huge step in a journey that might be challenging at times but will be many times more rewarding and fulfilling. That is why being prepared is so important.

Good Luck!

Register for Free Updates and More Practice Test Questions

Register your purchase at
https://www.test-preparation.ca/register/
for updates, free test tips and more practice test questions.

https://www.facebook.com/CompleteTestPreparation/

https://www.youtube.com/user/MrTestPreparation

CPSIA information can be obtained
at www.ICGtesting.com
Printed in the USA
LVHW040217290323
742932LV00011B/93